A Cottage Idyll

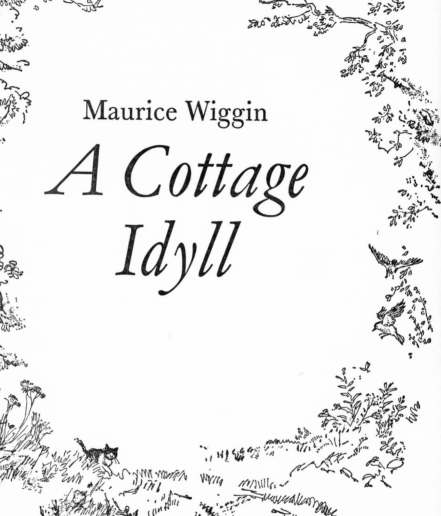

Maurice Wiggin

A Cottage Idyll

Nelson

THOMAS NELSON AND SONS LTD
36 Park Street London W1
P.O. Box 336 Apapa Lagos
P.O. Box 25012 Nairobi
P.O. Box 21149 Dar es Salaam
P.O. Box 2187 Accra
77 Coffee Street San Fernando Trinidad

THOMAS NELSON (AUSTRALIA) LTD
597 Little Collins Street Melbourne 3000

THOMAS NELSON AND SONS (SOUTH AFRICA)
(PROPRIETARY) LTD
51 Commissioner Street Johannesburg

THOMAS NELSON AND SONS (CANADA) LTD
81 Curlew Drive Don Mills Ontario

PRINTED IN GREAT BRITAIN BY
WESTERN PRINTING SERVICES LTD, BRISTOL

To
Robert and Doris Bowern
cottagers courageous
and compassionate
this book
is affectionately dedicated

Contents

 **I**

The view from from Tea-Cosy Cottage

It isn't called Tea-Cosy Cottage now; I'm not absolutely sure that the Post Office ever knew it by that name, though they may well have done. But that is what all the older inhabitants of the hamlet called it, and you could quite see how, with the original thatch waving down over the eaves in wayward undulations, it had earned its local name. Like the name, the cottage was almost absurdly picturesque.

Actually it pre-dated the English use of tea by quite a century or two. It was, the estate agent said firmly, Elizabethan. He was in no better position to prove it than we were in to disprove it, but it was certainly antique, emphatically Tudor, almost flamboyantly olde-worlde. And of course we had no wish to argue a point of provenance. We fell in love with it at first sight. And we thought we detected a response: though that, of course, may have been sheer sentimentality.

A house is inarticulate but it is not dumb. A new house may take some years to find its voice (though I have known some that were precocious). An old house always has something to say to one who will listen. True, some old houses seem indifferent: bored, it may well be, crushed by the boredom of entertaining generations of unappreciative lodgers. But many old houses, if not most, speak with an unmistakable voice, either hostile and malevolent, or warm and welcoming.

Tea-Cosy Cottage greeted us kindly. There was no doubt about it. Here I am (it said), not much to look at nor very handy, but sound and at your service. Take me as you find me. You are welcome.

We heard this voice. We knew then that we had come home, after much wandering and many strange roosts.

My wife Kay and I are both cottagers by inheritance, though in fact this was the first genuine cottage we had lived in in all our married life. But the roots were deep in the cottage mould. Country cottages in Shropshire, Worcestershire, and Cornwall all made their contribution: though our childhood was almost urban, we were continually visiting cottages in the deep tranquillity of the real countryside, where ancestral relatives still lived lives of profound simplicity and peace. (My wife's father was born in Minsterley, and his mother in Marazion.) We ourselves had lived in several urban houses and flats, but during the war, while I was in the R.A.F., we had made some sort of home whenever we had the chance; strange and sometimes poignant homes, lodging in remote farmhouses and cottages within cycling distance of the various airfields on which I served. Now it was time to put down roots, and after years of searching and longing we had stumbled on Tea-Cosy Cottage, and what the old cottage suggested, in its unassertive voice, was that this was the time and the place to put them down.

True, it was not precisely what I had carried in the mind's eye during long years of wandering and waiting. Perhaps the realization never quite squares with the dream. I had seen ever before the mind's eye that wild proud line of the Welsh hills, seen from the Shropshire side, or somewhere near the border of Hereford. It was a vague dream, but its essential qualities were clear. The smoke from my dream cottage drifted up out of a green and crooked valley against the standing wall of machicolated rock that is the March of Wales.

Tea-Cosy Cottage stands in another part of England, a fair march from the lonely sheep runs and secretive valleys of the dream. But what the reality lacked in grandeur and withdrawal it made up for in comeliness and cosiness. It was, and it is, a homely and buxom sort of land, soft of contour, in all things modest and moderate: a small-scale yet profound rusticity with its own quiet and apparently inviolable charm.

And the cottage, too – I have called it picturesque, which of course it is; yet it is not so very striking, superficially. You could drive past it quite unimpressed, only wondering, perhaps, that so casually planned a pile should have survived the storms of centuries. I would not even call it handsome. But when you come to live in it you learn its secret face.

It took us some time to learn its little ways – even to learn our way about it. Was there ever an interior more oddly arranged? Very likely its unplanned character comes from its curious history. It was built as a modest yeoman's house way back, doubtless in the sixteenth century, as the estate agent swore. There are little details which seem to confirm his faith. In the bad times following the Enclosures it was divided into two tiny labourer's cottages, and so it remained until our own time. Now it is once more one house – still a yeoman's house, I like to think – and its unhandy intricacies are the mark of its chequered past. We soon came to love the trick it has of showing you a luring view through every one of its many doors.

The informality of its plan (to use the most charitable term) means that every errand – for a mislaid book, a scuttle of coal, a basket of logs, a cup of tea – becomes a small adventure in the aesthetics of domestic design. Wherever you choose to stand you are in a nook that has a character of its own, and when you look out of it you see another corner, different in character, yet somehow complementary. And by some happy accident, or quirk of genius, the variety of the parts adds up to a whole that is all of one piece, stamped with personality, and not exactly like any other home. Though, to be sure, it is deeply rooted in the rural English tradition.

All this we sniffed at, half-seen and no more than suspected; yet *felt* with a deep certainty that somehow changed us and changed the day. We went away in a trance through the mellow October sunshine, and we knew that the next time we saw it we should see our home. Tea-Cosy Cottage had made us welcome.

*   *   *   *

First you check up on the ghosts, then you check up on the vermin, then you check up on the space available for storing books. Well, I don't say with utter certainty that that is a wife's full and exhaustive list of checks, but it is mine. Once satisfied on those three points I'm ready to move in. Assuming the roof doesn't leak too badly, there's not much else to worry about.

We were quite happy about the ghost situation. The old place radiated geniality. It wasn't particularly *light*: by the standards of horrible modernity, the goldfish bowl standard, it was probably rather dark. Yet not excessively so. Let us say it was private. The windows were small, but plentiful; and I would always prefer that to few and enormous. The cottage faces north-east, which by modern standards is eccentric. In fact it is perfect. Do you really want the blazing sun of high summer belting in through vast sheet-glass windows? We don't: we go out when we want the sun, we come in when we want to insulate ourselves a little from the extremes of nature. And we like our bit of privacy.

The situation gave us a cool, big living room (two knocked into one: a room in which indeed we lived, and ate, and often worked) yet the fact that there were all these little windows poked in almost everywhere where there was a bit of vacant wall between the beams gave us sufficient sunlight all the day round from dawn to sunset. In winter it was pretty snug. The interior walls are of rough brick, which we regularly painted white, and a great quantity of blackened oak beams made an irregular and fascinating pattern. The ceiling, devilish low, is likewise a forest of black beams. This old style of domestic architecture isn't to everybody's taste, of course – it doesn't have the soothing proportions of Georgian, the aristocratic spaciousness – but it is beguiling and cosy.

I can say with some fervour that when you've lived with Tudor beamy for a dozen years or so, nothing else seems quite right. This is not the view of Beverley Nichols, I know, and I don't for a moment contest the view that Georgian was the apogee of English domestic, the nonpareil, the summit whence all since has been a sad decline. However, there are temperaments to which cosy Tudor beamy makes a profound appeal, when even the recurrent thump of bonce against beams, the endless stealthy accretion of dust, the permanent stoop and shuffle which this style imposes, seem small prices to pay for the unforced felicity of the design.

And of course Georgian implies a standard of living, a spacious well-heeled pattern which includes servants and affluent amplitude, to which we never aspired. We are cottagers at heart.

Well, we were satisfied that there were no ghosts at Tea-Cosy

A Cottage Idyll

Cottage, or, perhaps I should say, that the resident ghosts were genial and quiet. You can tell in a trice. As for vermin, there appeared to be none. We were by way of being specialists in mice, and not without experience of bats and cockroaches. Our first London flat, in Maida Hill, was infested with 'roaches'. Once in Wales we lodged in a house which was more or less a cavern of bats. As for mice, our summit experience also came in Wales, when we had a flat in an ancient farmhouse with a total absence of all mod. cons. It was here that we lived for a year or two in rather primitive conditions, which, such is the buoyancy of youth, not only failed to depress us, but actually confirmed us in a predilection for the so-called simple life. The privy was way down at the bottom of the vegetable garden – quite a trip in the dark of a rainy winter's night. Indeed, on one occasion, when Kay had borrowed my gumboots to make the journey, she slipped on the muddy path and lay among the wet cabbages for quite a time, struggling, like a Kelly, to regain her feet, and uttering faint cries. All water had to be gained from the pump in the farmyard and carried within: we washed, and washed-up, our 'flat' being merely two upstairs rooms, at a bowl on a marble-topped wash-hand-stand. For illumination we had an oil lamp and two candle-sticks. On the open fire we burned nothing but wood, which we had to gather, in the fields and spinneys. This was pretty well irreducibly simple as a way of life, but none the worse for that, though I don't suppose we would really like to go back to it now. But it was good practice for the way of life we had in mind when the war should end. And here, in this Welsh Eden, we battled with mice on a scale unknown before or since.

To say that we were infested is the simple truth. The walls were apparently hollow, and troupes of mice galloped up and down within them, making a sound, magnified as it was, like horses. They emerged whenever they felt they could do so with impunity, through so many cracks and crevices that we despaired, and rightly, of ever stopping them up. Every night we set several traps in the living room: before we had properly got undressed and into bed, in the adjoining room, we heard them going off. In the morning, when I came to clear out the ashes and re-light the fire, mice ran out from the warm crevices of ancient brickwork in which they had been enjoying a cosy doze. No cat could live in that house, for some strange reason which we never discovered. Several tried; all pined away. Cats throve in the farm buildings, but not indoors. It was as if the mice carried in their bloodstream some long-term, racial immunity – individuals died to the cats, but then the cats fell sick, and the race of mice throve. It was all rather sad and disturbing, and I will not pretend that we were not glad to leave. Enough is enough.

Tea-Cosy Cottage was free of vermin. It had been thoroughly gutted and 'gone-over' during certain minimal alterations which were said to have 'modernized' it, though in a pretty sketchy way. The thatch had been replaced, many years before, by tiles, thereby removing one major source of vermin-infestation. The downstairs floors had been re-laid, in a highly slapdash fashion, the walls and skirtings sealed off against invasion. It was clear. Just in one aspect, which wholly failed to trouble us, there was a trace of lodgers.

The east wall of the little house is hung with tiles. The winds that blow from Prussia and all the barbarous East boom against them in vain. You would say at a glance, seeing the cottage from afar, that these titles were red. But when you get close you see that the lower half of each is a living surface of most delicate pale green. Each is a miniature garden. It is a miracle worked by English rain and air. It is lichen, a symbiosis of fungi and algae; the spontaneous generation that you rarely see in cities or in the acid air of the industrial north.

Behind these tiles a few bats had their residence. One in particular we came to know quite well, in that first autumn in

A Cottage Idyll

Tea-Cosy Cottage. In the late afternoon, if it were fine, a little pipistrelle would dart out from his home under the eaves and chase frantically around, snapping up insects that still danced briefly in the mild air before sunset.

His hour of opportunity shrank daily; soon there would be nothing for him but the long precarious sleep. To tiny creatures living rough in hedgerow and coppice the first cold nights must come as a mortal shock.

Knowing these things and unable quite to forget them, you relish the lucky chance by which you were born human. Alone of living things you have the mastery over nightfall and yearfall, and the certain knowledge of dawn and spring. You draw the curtains over darkening windows on which a splat of cold rain rattles, and as you turn towards the hearth familiar homely things seem beautiful.

On this east wall only, the prudential carapace of red-green tiles comes down from the rooftree like a coat of mail, and stops short at the top of a window. Behind this window is where I sometimes sit and write, and sometimes just sit and watch our neighbours the birds. There was one in particular, a blue tit, whom I spotted one day early on, in the act of flying home to the snuggery he had made just above my window, under the tiles. We got to know one another quite well. When I felt companionable, and could spare the time, he sat on one of the bars of my window – his doorstep, so to speak – and looked in on me. I wonder what he made of it.

Looking in, he could see a desk, a typewriter, a litter of papers, fishing rods ranged in a rack, pictures on the wall, countless books. It took me much more than a bird's lifetime to accumulate all this stuff, but I doubt if the blue tit would be impressed. The thought suddenly struck me: Perhaps he thinks I am in a cage.

The thought was absurdly difficult to shake off.

That was a perverse bird, that blue tit. He had an unnatural fondness for paper work. Our morning papers are rolled up and thrust into the top bar of the gate, and if nobody got there before him this blue tit was sure to be there pecking away at *The Times*. I could understand his having a go at milk cartons (not that there *were* any milk cartons in our life) but *The Times*. . . .

If we were clear of ghosts and vermin, emphatically we were blessed by birds. Now began a phase of our lives in which the daily company of birds was our beatitude.

I love birds. Big birds, little birds, likely birds and highly unlikely birds. The whole crazy alphabet of birds. I dote on the dotterel, the dipper, the dunlin. There is room in my life for the wryneck, the roller, the reeve. For the whimbrel, the whooper, the widgeon. For the whilk and the Willy Wicket. For gargany, goosander, gannet. For the smew, the scaup, the shoveller and the shag.

The rainbow of birds . . . Black-necked grebe, red-necked phalarope, white-eyed pochard, yellow-brown warbler, purple heron, tawny pipit, roseate tern, honey-buzzard, ruddy sheldrake and great grey shrike.

Birds geographical . . . Siberian chiff-chaff, Bahama pintail, Greenland redpoll, Lapland larkspur, African yellowbill, French partridge, Manx shearwater, Canada goose.

Birds biographical . . . the proprietary or sponsored birds . . . Montagu's harrier, Wilson's snipe, Temminck's stint. Baillon's crake, Buffont's skua, Scop's owl, Richard's pipit, and the storm petrel which sailors used to call Mother Carey's Chicken.

Birds fantastical, birds poetical . . . Pick-cheese, pyewipe, pratincole. Hoopoe, hobby, hoodie. Bonxie, boomer, bosun. Praise be for the bartailed godwit, the squacco heron, the ferruginous duck.

We had not been resident at Tea-Cosy Cottage for twenty-four hours before we saw a pheasant, a glorious cock, strolling nonchalantly in the cabbage patch, and the great green wood-pecker, Yaffle, the emperor, swooping in all glorious to peck away at a willow tree for a few minutes before he disappeared in a flash of scarlet and emerald. Within a day or two we had located our other regulars – a pair of jays, no friend to the toiling gardener but far too glorious a bird to dislike; a lesser spotted woodpecker, rather less shy than Yaffle but still imperiously private; a pair of goldfinches, a pair of pied wagtails which walked daily on the lawn; the wren and the robin, the permanent troupe of starlings, sparrows both house and hedge, thrushes, blackbirds, and the odd warbler. Lap-wings and fieldfares visited near, that first winter; there was an abundance of finches; and most affectionate, naughty, mis-chievous and cocky of them all, the lovable tits.

Bold or shy, there is company for a quiet day and colour for a grey day in the bright breviary of birds.

Autumn

The cottage diary began in autumn, of all seasons the most rewarding for the diarist. There is ceaseless change to note, leisure to record it, and above all there is that benign influence of the equinox which brings out the philosopher in us all; the tremor of irreversible change which calls for all the charity, all the benevolence, all the stoicism in one's nature. All seasons bring their meed of happiness to the born cottager living an arm's-length from the ineluctable mystery of hedgerow and coppice, the unlegislated fervour of the wild; but autumn finds him best disposed to remember his own trespasses, and to forgive.

*   *   *   *

A Cottage Idyll

Four times a day we hear flying feet racing up or down the lane. Suddenly they stop, and there is a heavy silence. Looking out of one of the cottage's tiny windows, with due discretion, we see small boys earnestly scrutinizing pavement, gutter and hedgerow under the great old walnut tree by the gate. It stands in our orchard and is technically 'our' tree, but it massively overhangs the lane and this provides problems and opportunities which enrich the lives of small boys, providing them with an early introduction to the complex ethics of human society.

Unwontedly pensive and studious, they peer and shuffle among the thickening mat of fallen leaves. Sometimes they spot us watching them, and then, with a most uncharacteristic access of shyness, they race away, to school or home, according to the time of day. Bolder spirits return later to throw sticks up into the old Blenheim apple tree that overlooks Back Lane, safely out of sight of the cottage windows. But I could name every one of them. Nobody stirs in the village without being seen, identified, and reported. If the nation's intelligence service were half so good as the village's, there would be nothing to fear.

I cannot work up much moral indignation about a crime which I have committed so often. Philosophically we gather up the sticks that have been hurled into the orchard. They come in handy for kindling. Finding enough kindling is a problem peculiar to those who keep open fires in cottages. There is never enough. One becomes a scrounger, with a sharp eye for free fuel: no walk is taken without this ulterior motive. It gives the least parsimonious of us a solacing sense of thrift.

Only once did I feel a slight touch of choler about the boys, when one scoundrel sent me a roundabout and diplomatic message to the effect that he would like his cherished scrumping stick back. Apparently it had served him well as a sort of boomerang – at any rate until this unfortunate incident, which he blamed obscurely on the gnarled state of my unpruned

branches, a disgrace to the village. He let it be understood
that on this sad occasion some other wretch had 'had a lend
of it'. I'm afraid he will get on famously in the world, that
boy.

To fair-weather fishermen, scrumping time is rather sad. It
marks the end of their short season. They take to swapping
fishing books, with which to prolong, in imagination, the season
which they themselves abbreviate in fact. Others, like my
friend Bill Cumper and me, employ subtler devices for perpetu-
ating summer. Bill is a creative genius who made a television
set with his own hands at a time when most of us had never
even heard of it. He is up to that sort of trick, a man at home
in a world that is pure black magic to my innocent mind – a
mind innocent of electricity, I mean. There is almost nothing in
the electronic line that he does not understand, that he cannot
master. That is the sort of man I have for friend. I do not
know what I have done to deserve it, I who can barely solder a
joint. And I do not inquire. One takes life's gifts gratefully, as
they come.

Bill and I prolong the season by an elaborate game of
bartering fishing tackle. Ostensibly, Bill arrives to adjust my
television set, but there is a bland and tacit understanding that
this is only a front for other and infinitely more interesting
subjects, such as photography, home-made wine, salmon and
sailing boats. However, we observe an almost Chinese ritual
of oblique reference, and when the currently negotiable reel
or rod is brought out, one is expected to show surprise.

Of course, it is but a short step from the lip-pursing and
head-shaking of negotiation to a trial cast on the lawn. This
is the point at which Kay usually intervenes, with a tactful
reminder that there are television sets waiting to be repaired,
and words waiting to be written. And, to do her justice, tea
waiting to be drunk.

I doubt if either Bill or I could live to an office routine.

A Cottage Idyll

The essence of being your own master is that you work hard when you work, but in your own time; you take your own risks, set your own standards, and play when you feel like playing. Of course, it's all right for sensible wives to remind you occasionally of the minor realities of life; so long as they don't do it too often, don't begin to confuse minor realities with major; but by and large you must be independent of clock and calendar, a maverick in the original sense that you bear no man's proprietorial brand. Otherwise what is the point in being your own master? Bill and I both work darned hard when there's work to be done, but if we fancy a cup of tea and a rattle about fishing, we indulge that fancy. Then, of course, you have to catch up. It may mean staying up half the night. Never mind. The essential thing is to reserve your freedom, and the dignity that comes of downing tools to honour the immemorial dues of friendship.

*   *   *   *

Not a breath of wind. The fragrant smoke of burning leaves goes straight up and is lost in the veil of mist. There will be fog tonight.

Smog is a drab word for a drab thing, but fog used to be romantic. Or perhaps romance, like beauty, is in the eye of the beholder? I speak now of a time long past, before smog and middle age had been invented. It was once a lovely thing to walk the city streets in fog. You met surprising people. You made friends. You might even fall in love.

I have known it to happen.

People are human and loving in time of tribulation. Drama releases something spontaneous that is locked up within routine. While you are young you want drama all the time; as you grow older you come to prefer routine. But it is the drama that humanizes and invigorates; when there is a little mild danger or change that affects all equally. Or even a great danger. But it must be arbitrary and equal. It must be something impartial and inescapable about which you can feel innocent. Something natural and neutral, like fog. Then the cold protective mask comes off. For a time. I knew of a happy marriage that stemmed from a chance meeting of strangers in a fog. The children are beautiful. And I knew of a stormy, star-crossed love affair that had the same beginning. But a different ending.

Scenting the coming of fog I fell to thinking about the lurid and laughable chanciness of human affairs. Life is a gamble, though some find it pleasant and reassuring to think otherwise. Let them be. There is no point in trying to dodge your destiny. The end is in the beginning. Stars, gods, or genes . . . call it what you like, chemistry or morality, it makes no odds, you are what you are. I find this thought inescapable and consoling.

This afternoon I spent an hour sitting on a log by a fire in the orchard, stripping runner beans out of the old pods and inhaling the aromatic scent of burning leaves and twigs. By rights the seed beans for next year should still be hanging on the vine, slowly drying out as the sap goes down. But this year we used a curious silky-stranded sort of string with which to lash the interlacing wigwam of bean poles. No one will confess to actually buying the stuff, but someone did. The birds were on to it in a flash. They tugged and tugged and carried away yards of silky fibres to line their nests. It was a luxury to them. Word got around among the sparrow community that here was a line in house furnishing that was well worth a journey. One result was that all the sparrows seemed unusually chirpy. Another was that the first good equinoctial blow weakened the bean-pole structure so seriously that I had to dismantle it over-early.

When I had stripped the seed beans out of the pods I took them indoors to dry off gently in a colander on the hearth stone. Thank heaven ours is a house wherein nobody thinks it odd or

eccentric to see a colander of seed beans on the hearth. I've
seen stranger things there.

*   *   *   *

I am writing this on my own hearth, in a quiet room, at the end
of the day. They say there will be gales before morning.
Tonight we lit the first ceremonious fire of autumn. It is dying
now, but not long ago logs blazed and crackled under the
black canopy and threw a ruddy dancing light on the white-
washed walls of the inglenook.

I sat in a high-backed chair with my feet to the flames and
savoured the smells of tobacco and wood smoke, and Kay sat
sewing by lamplight, and we spoke of storms, and the old cat
laid his head on the kerb and slept. He is sleeping yet, and now
it is all done, the work of the day and the pleasure.

The pleasure so various . . . Food eaten together in conviviality,
blessed by friendship; the long trudge on the river bank; the
sweating and the reading, the talking and the singing. Now I
am alone with the end of it: fire dying and wind rising.

Soon I must make the rounds of the house. I know what I
shall find. This is peaceful country. I make the rounds for the
pleasure of recognition, expecting neither ghost nor thief.

At this time of year, the fire lighting time, I shall find
particular fresh evidence of autumn. In my own small room,
ranged on top of the bookcases with the reels and the line-
driers and the jolly painted floats, there will be the first of that
fine array of little jars in which the winter's baits are preserved
in sugar or glycerine or a solution of formaldehyde. Minnows,
sand eels, gudgeon, loaches, sprats both gold and silver,
prawns and elderberries and stewed wheat. This is the minor
harvest of the all-the-year-round angler.

In kitchen and larder I shall see Kay's handiwork, damsons
and gooseberries and rhubarb in their wide-necked glass jars,
and the vast old-fashioned stone jars and jorums of salted

beans and rosy red cabbage. Last year's pickled walnuts are right and ready now, which is just as well, for this year the old tree has given us none.

An early summer drought finished off the currants and raspberries, too, but there are fragrant bunches of thyme and lavender, ready to go into their little linen bags to keep winter sweet. The potatoes are boxed up and the onions strung high and dry. It is the larder of a woman who is glad to be 'just' a housewife. Heaven be praised.

When I have finished the little ritual of my 'rounds' I shall go out and have a look at the night and sniff the wind. It is long odds that the village will be sleeping and not a light showing on the Downs. If there is any sound above that of the rising wind in the elms, it will be the owl calling, or an unquiet cow with her mind on maternity.

This is the peace at the day's end for which, in an evil time, so many nights were made intolerable. I shall lock the door and take my book to bed, conscious of history and happiness and a rising wind.

* * * *

I woke at 3 a.m. from a dream of artillery fire. The heavens were burning again over Normandy; in the bloody lee of Caen each slit trench held its strung tension of hope and fear. It took me a moment to realize that the war was only the wind, thumping the old casement, which is slightly shaky. The first gale of autumn had arrived on time.

On the little bedside table there was a copy of Montaigne's *Essays*, the *Collected Poems* of W. H. Auden, *The Motor Cycle*, *A Fresh Water Stream* by my great friend Henry Williamson, *Fishing Gazette*, and a folder advertising life insurance which had been craftily inserted in one of those publications by a cunning salesman who wanted to frighten me into trading the present for the future.

A Cottage Idyll

I took this insurance advertisement and with some glee folded it thick and rammed it into the window frame, pleased to find a use for something so useless. That stopped the rattling, but by now, of course, we were all wide awake. We wondered if the little cats in the kitchen would be scared by the gale, for they had never heard a gale before.

I went down the narrow twisting staircase feeling good, for I rather like being woken up in the middle of the night provided I can get back to bed. The furry brothers were sound asleep, as it happened, but they too like being woken in the middle of the night, and we had a little party. I poured a drop of milk and warmed it, very slightly, and they had a sip apiece and washed their tousled little faces and began to dash around like mad things.

I rounded them up, eventually, after they had sneaked into the study and had a friendly wrestle on my desk, scattering papers like chaff, and although they gazed at me reproachfully when I dumped them gently on their bed, they still wore that enchanting tousled look and I knew they would soon be sound-O again.

I lay awake for a while, pleased to eavesdrop on the mysterious night, reading and sipping and smoking, listening to the gale and gradually sinking into slumber, and the last thing I remember thinking was that next morning would see the trees stripped bare. In fact they were not, though the old walnut had dropped a few more crisp and brittle leaves on the cropped grass of the orchard. The countryside was calm again and it looked no different, except that it was clean and fresh and somehow expectant.

But this was a proclamation of autumn, a proclamation with trumpets, and thereafter, however subtly, life was changed. When the day's work was done I gathered kindling, and cut apple logs, which smell so sweet, and a few of beech, which blaze merrily, and while I was getting them I felt the first nip in the air.

Autumn

We lit the fire ceremoniously, and when it fell dark we did not light a lamp but sat and watched the brilliant and tender flames dancing on the whitewashed old bricks of the chimney corner.

So autumn came, with its promise of small but succulent joys which never fail . . . Great golden scrubbed potatoes going into the oven to bake; big cheery apples; chestnuts, hot toddy, mulled ale; logs a-burning, bare beautiful trees, bonfires, long walks in the woods. And above all, the simple and supreme pleasure of coming home.

That is what I chiefly like about autumn: with all its sadness, it restores the fireside to its proper primacy. Human aspirations are strange and complex, but a happy hearth is the summit of human felicity. And this you enjoy most keenly in the first evenings of autumn.

At any rate, this is true of me, October-born, stimulated by storm, variable as weather, delighting in contrast and the sublime core of changelessness at the heart of change.

*   *   *   *

We took a sack today and went to gather bracken. This is one of the important ritual engagements of the year. We slipped through a gap in the hedge, entered the coppice, and in half a dozen paces we had lost the modern world. A car went purring down the lane within twenty yards and it was invisible, as unrelated to our world as a silly old satellite whizzing aimlessly through the uninhabitable nightmare of space.

The bracken was warm to the touch, though the afternoon was cool and grey. There is a quality of innate or residual warmth in the curling ruddy fronds that matches their brave colour.

You have to be careful. The stems grow tough and hard, not round but angular in section, quite capable of cutting flesh. And often you find that you have grasped a briar. But what is a wood without a briar? We were both brought up on Walter de la Mare. Some say it is sentimental slush:

> Very old are the woods,
> And the buds that break
> Out of the briar's boughs
> When March winds wake
> So old with their beauty are,
> O, no man knows
> Through what wild centuries
> Roves back the rose.

It is very nearly impossible to write like that now. But I don't know about its being sentimental slush.

The light drained slowly out of the sky and we tied the neck of the sack and left the wood. Eyes watched us all the way. Squirrel and magpie, rabbit and pheasant marked our progress, and as we reached the lane again rooks were flying home across the ploughland, and they saw us too.

The bracken is for mulching shrubs. There is nothing like it for keeping frost out and moisture in, heaped around the little stems of trunk and spread around over the roots in golden circles like huge squandered coins.

It is mainly for the azaleas that we fetch bracken. They are almost our only concession to exoticism in an old-fashioned English cottage garden. They need encouragement and support, as if they felt the strangeness of a foreign land. They are anything but precocious. The shy blooms of the young shrubs merely hint at the flamboyance, the flaunting glory that is to come, one day, when they shall have settled down in English soil and accepted the companionship of roses. So we cosset them a little. Not too much – it is no use being soft with growing things. We never use artificial aids to propagation. Nature is rough and tough and callous and you can't interpolate the compassionate methods of the Welfare State. Green and growing things must survive if they can, on their own terms, the terms of their ingrained endurance, their inbred vitality and will to live. And in any case, what happens if you go finicking about, forcing things early? In the end you have everything starting a week earlier than your neighbour – and finishing a week earlier, too. You might just as well let the natural rhythm of the seasons prevail. There is a time for birth and a time for death.

It is the time for making fast against winter. Squirrel and hedgehog, gardener and smallholder, all are busy to the same purpose. But for us, this year, there is one job the fewer to do. Bracken alone will suffice, this winter, to protect the tiny dwarf conifer, still only eight inches high, which Kay has been cherishing for a year. *Thuya occidentalis ellwangeriana aurea*: the golden midget with a giant name. Last winter it needed its little screen of hessian stretched on sticks to keep it snug from the nor'-easters. From our window we could see it nestling in its shelter, but passers-by were curious.

'What's that you've got behind the 'erden?' asked a man from the midlands; and my heart gave a jump. I hadn't heard hessian called herden since I was a boy, in the days of the Saturday penny and the sticklebacks, and buttercups and daisies gathered like treasure in ragged little fields between the pit heads and the smoking heaps of slag.

*   *   *   *

Now is the time for walking in the orchard in the cool, sweet evening. The cropped grass is starred with fallen apples, and the trees droop like willows under the weight of fruit.

Perhaps 'orchard' is a grandiloquent word for a little plot with just two dozen trees, most of them old and gnarled. But what else can you call it? And who would want another name? Orchard is one of the loveliest words.

It is one of that company of evocative and potent nouns that work a spell. Different nouns work magic for different people:

A Cottage Idyll

perhaps our favourite words tell something about us. Make a list
of the things you like best, and that is poetry for *you* . . .

Orchard, autumn, lake, landfall, estuary, evening, forest, frost,
fireside, rain, dawn, hawthorn, harbour, valley, shore, island,
blossom, swallow, willow, weir, windfall . . .

Windfalls. We gather them up by the basketful. Soon it will be
time to hire young boys to climb the trees. It seems a preposterous
thing, no doubt, but there is a certain cunning in it. For this
stratagem, though expensive, assures me a fair portion of my
crop, and it removes temptation from the lives of the boys, and it
sets their kind in a mercantile way of thinking, which will be
valuable to them later on, in this wicked world.

I would do it myself, of course, but I have no head for heights.
And if you have no head for heights, then climbing up into an
apple tree will unsettle you just as surely as climbing a steeple
or a tall mast shrouded in rigging that thrashes and whistles in
the wind. All this, they say, comes of having been badly brought
up, in one way or another. I do not believe it for a moment. When
I was a boy I had a good head for heights, and quite a fair head
for figures, and a little later on – not much later – I had a good
head for wine. All these qualities have gone from me now.

Well, the boys will climb my trees, that are so old and gnarled
but still bearing countless apples. They are not the most distin-
guished apples, any more than their owner is the most distin-
guished apple eater; but they are well enough. There are eaters
called Blenheim, which mature slowly and survive long, coming
to their prime at Christmas, and a cooker called Booker, passable
in a pie. I shall give the boys a miserly reward (after all, I am
paying them for their pleasure) and lay out the apples in long
rows to mellow with the advance of autumn. Everyone concerned
will be pleased and profited. There are few business deals of which
you can say so much.

It is not easy to sustain a cynical or a suspicious turn of mind

36

when the apple crop is coming in. To earn this crop I have done almost nothing; apart from a little rudimentary and half-hearted pruning, nothing at all. Except perhaps that I have stood under the trees in winter and loved them when they were at their barest. Anyone can love them in blossom time, but you have to take a tree for better and for worse. Time and again I have paused by the bole of a tree and laid my ear to its rough bark, listening for the murmur of its blood, inhaling its patience and its will.

The apples are far ahead of the elms this autumn. They are ripe and ready and falling in every breath of wind on to the cropped grass, while the elms are still quite green. Just here and there in the tall wall of solid green there is a dusting of gold. It is like a man who begins to go grey at the temples: some think he is at his best then. I am sure of it.

Maturity is ripeness, and ripeness is all. True, it has its sadness, but not so bitterly sad as the extreme poignant sadness of youth.

When I was out the other day with my friend Alan, the farmer, in a little boat on the estuary, we saw a flight of wild geese, a beautiful elongated arrowhead of geese caught in their own mysterious compulsions, flying south. There were other signs, too. We caught neither bass nor eels – they are all offshore now, in deeper, warmer water, following the pull of their natures. The flat fish were still there, the non-migratory flounders, which live all the year round in the tidal creek, sparrows of the sea. They are fatter than plaice or soles and their flesh is darker, less delicate; but you grow to enjoy them. Ideally a flounder needs a bit of bacon on the side, or, at least, it should be cooked in bacon fat. Breakfast today: flounder caught in the creek, mushrooms picked in the meadow, bacon grown on Alan's farm. After we had beaten back up to the quay, a laborious business against the ebb tide, there all around us were boats being laid up for the winter. Some find these signs saddening. They feel the spirit shrinking

37

within them. But autumn, like middle age, has its compensations. There is no point in telling you what they are, for if you are middle aged you know already, and if you are young you will not believe them.

To my regret, there is only one pear tree in our little orchard. But next month we shall plant another, and that will be an occasion. I would rather plant a tree than anything that grows. A tree will keep you company, it modifies the landscape subtly, and it will survive you, carrying a trace of your design and will into the future you will not see. Already in our small plot we have raised the sacred rowan, willow, beech, birch, oak, laburnum and walnut. This last is an act of faith indeed. The great tree which it replaces was sixty feet high, and heaven knows how old, when it fell. The age of the remaining great walnut by the gate we know precisely. It was planted in 1815, the year of Waterloo. Most of the walnut trees in the village were taken down in that year, to make gunstocks. There is always a link with the past, a link with history, if you care to find it. We are not so lonely as we sometimes feel.

Kay says that the new pear tree should be either a William or a Conference. In that case it will be a William. William is a fine friendly, homely name. I could not eat a Conference with equal pleasure; at least, I should not come to it with equal anticipation. Conference is a bad name for a sensual pleasure; an absurd name. Its associations are ugly. Names matter, and so they should. They are not only part of things, they are sometimes the spirit of things.

My friend Fred Heather is lucky in his name. Fred is our local plumber, and the most distinguished-looking man for miles around. He has a high forehead and a military bearing, yet perhaps not quite military, in the overbearing sense; more high-academical. When he stoops to inspect a tap he puts on gold pince-nez. When he rides through the village on his bicycle he looks like a don riding to lecture.

Autumn

I am always glad to luff up and have a chat with Fred Heather, for he finds life amusing, and although a plumber must see people at their worst, he has the gift of tolerance. September and for that matter October too make it a little easier to be tolerant, I find. It is usually rather nice to be rid of August, which is neither fresh summer nor exciting autumn: a cruel month, lowering, thundery, dusty, drab, featureless and forlorn. The spirit lifts with the coming of the equinoctial excitements.

When the evening is all woodsmoke and the faint keen smell of apples, it is good to stand under the trees, in an English village, savouring the bitter-sweet second-best of the year.

*   *   *   *

The wind rose and the sun came out and the world changed. It happened in a moment. Before this happened everything and everybody had been grey.

Three children were playing a listless game in a patch of rough grass that is railed off from the road, just across the way from Tea-Cosy Cottage. The village pond used to be here, but somebody filled it in, years ago. As if a village can be complete or happy without a pond. So now it is always waterlogged and every winter men come from 'the Council' with a lorry and dig improvised or *ad hoc* drains to get the water away.

Small pond creatures still haunt the ghost of a pond, as if their ancestral memories impelled them. The biggest boy had caught a bright green frog. The boy hated the grey dank day and the pondlessness of life; and he took his revenge on the frog.

A man passing by hated the dank grey day and the emptiness of life and he made the boy set the frog free, though perhaps he did not really care whether the frog was happy or sad so long as the boy got a taste of his own disillusionment.

The boy hated the man so much he was blind with anger and he banged his head on the iron rail. He clapped his hands to the bruise and when the pain grew manageable he attacked his small companions and they all went down into the sodden grass, screaming and hating.

The frog crept away, too simple to hate.

In the misty orchard a man with a scythe swung doggedly at the humpy wet grass. It slid away from the blade and the blade caught on a stone and the man swore.

He walked to the hedge like a beaten man and picked up the rubbing stone and sharpened his scythe again, with slow sad strokes.

A woman trudged down to the farm to fetch eggs. There was no one at home. The farm was deserted. She got mud on her shoes, and the cows mooned around looking at her with great stupid eyes and stood in her path, and she laddered a stocking, and as she walked back home she thought of mud and ladders and eggless teatime and the long littleness of life.

Then in one moment the wind rose and the sun came out. Birds that had been huddled in the dripping trees rose and wheeled and floated on the wind, all the birds of the village on the wing at once. The wind drove the grass on to the scythe and the sun gleamed on the blade.

The man with the scythe got out his pipe and filled it, and he lit it, and the blue smoke shirred away merrily. He watched for a moment the birds wheeling and floating, and he noticed that the golden elms were still green in places, although thousands of leaves were travelling on the wind. And he set to scything.

The little boys felt the wind cool on their hot faces, and they felt the greyness driven out of the day. They ran across the road to open the gate for the woman with·the empty egg basket. She gave them a coin, and they ran away chattering to the village shop. She smiled and went slowly through the orchard, enjoying the whistle of the scythe in the grass.

She sat for a moment on the old wooden chair at the kitchen door and she watched the birds dancing and the clouds racing,

swarming across the brilliant sky, and she listened to the golden
elms. Then she put on the copper kettle and it caught a gleam of
sunshine, and she began to sing.

*   *   *   *

I am an unspeakable creature, practically an untouchable.
Annoyed to find that I have a heavy cold, I take furiously to
healthy living. Late in the day, of course. Among these belated
virtuous steps, I eat raw onions, which are said to be full of
health. They are delicious, too. Decent brown bread, raw onion,
Caerphilly cheese, watercress and honey – what a wonderful
meal. But you can't eat raw onions and remain popular. Then I
eschew popularity. I am no good to anyone smelling nice and
feeling nasty. My nearest and dearest must put up with me
reeking of onions and earnings.

I love the vegetable world, though I have no exaggerated
belief in its healthfulness. I have sampled the cooking of many
nations. There is nothing, in my opinion, to touch the Chinese.
They treat the vegetable world with reverence. If I were rich I
would employ a Chinese cook.

But he would make a gambler of me. All Chinese are said to be
gamblers. Certainly the Chinese whom I have known fairly well
have been addicted to it. Though I know that life is a wild gamble
from start to finish, I rarely 'gamble' in the particular sense. I
adore poker but lose dramatically when I play it. I am told
that I have the opposite of a poker face. Can I correct this by
taking thought?

That reminds me, the poker needs mending. I broke it. Though
far from strong, I have broken more pokers than any man
breathing. They come to pieces in my hands. This is a melancholy
and inexplicable distinction.

Down the lane I met a man in a mist and we talked for a time
about the atom bomb, which, he assured me, caused the dirty
weather. He just conceivably could be right. Scientists blandly

41

laugh it off, but can you believe all those chaps say? Scientists have a vested interest in science.

There was suddenly a great commotion and squawking on the hidden lake. I said 'Is that the mallard?'

'Well,' he said, 'it ain't the Luton Girls' Choir.'

From logic's paralysing grip, let us be rescued, O Lord, by a saving sense of the absurd.

*   *   *   *

'Pheasant: per portion, 34*s*. 9*d*.' So it said on the menu in the grand restaurant. I thought that perhaps boldness would be the best policy, as it usually is, and pointed it out to my guest, using an incredulous and disapproving tone and hoping he would turn out to be a game old bird himself.

'Oh, well, then, we'll start off with two lots of that, shall we?' John said innocently. Luckily he is an old friend with a strong though slightly warped sense of humour. We had the mutton.

When I got back to the cottage that afternoon there were two cock pheasants in the garden, strolling among the cabbages and curly kale with the debonair arrogance that so often goes with innate stupidity. The temptation was terrible.

I have a notion that some lesser characters find the temptation altogether too strong. Several times when I have been sitting by the dying fire, late at night, I have heard the flat rattle of gunfire. It is wonderful what you can do with a lamp and a bit of resolution. Or so I hear. Pheasants, hand-reared in a super welfare state, lack the true wild bird's inborn suspicion of mankind. This is a time when gamekeepers, a suspicious breed of men, don't much like to hear the sound of a car being driven slowly along a lane, late at night.

The midnight fusillade, like the ragged but respectable gunfire of Saturday afternoons, when the so-called 'sportsmen' come down in their Bentleys and Jaguars and estate wagons – this is a sign of the time. It tells you as surely as a calendar that the date is November. A month which I can find lovable.

The trout have gone out of season, but grayling are still rising in the mildish middle of the day, and pike are just coming into their prime. There is no day of the year on which it is not good to fish, but I would almost as soon live through a November's day, spinning for pike, as an April day fly fishing for trout. Almost.

The robins have marked out their winter territory and are always ready to defend it, against real or imagined aggression, with a furious intransigence that is almost human. The hedge sparrows have made it plain which lengths of hedgerow they regard as their own, and the coal tits are beginning to raid the tops of milk bottles. And Christmas is coming.

All seasons have their enthusiasts. But November, the frontier in time between autumn and winter, is perhaps an acquired taste, like oysters and flounders and dry white wine. It is a month which can get you down if you do not react to it in a positive way. If you huddle up defensively and let it invest the citadel of your spirit, lay siege to your passive will, it can seem a melancholy time indeed. But if you accept the challenge and step out to see the sights, it becomes a rewarding month, full of subtle pleasures of its own.

I don't know what life offers that is lovelier than a flight of wild duck, seen against a pearly November sky. With blue mist mantling the distant ridge of downs, and a lighted window at the end of the lane.

2

3

Winter

In the dark forests of the north, long ago, lived strong, cruel, restless, reckless, hardy, handsome men.

In six adjectives I give you my deplorable ancestors; and possibly yours. They, too, were immodest and immoderate.

In summer they kept on the move, mainly by water, hunting and fishing and killing people for the pleasure of it. They abominated work. In the long terrible winter they stayed at home, huddled together in crude forts built of logs. They soon got on one another's nerves and the casualties of winter were almost as severe as the losses of the summer raids. They whiled away the time in eating and drinking swinishly, fighting, boasting, making love, and singing haunting heroic songs full of melancholy and bombast and enchanting lies.

They were a little mad.

But there were thinkers among them, mystics and mathematicians of a sort, who invented gods and ceremonies, without which no society manages to hang together. These magicians understood something of the meaning and mystery of the shortest day, or if not, they invented it. The winter solstice was the time of rites and feasts.

I have no particle of evidence that these bandits were my forbears. Except this kinship of feeling. For the solstice is a time which I, too, celebrate in my heart. It is the second best time of the whole year.

Now we have reached rock-bottom, the black pit and nadir of the year. All that follows must improve. Slowly and surely, now, the days will lengthen. Winter is on the retreat. Through bitter weather or mild, the light is winning, towards the next great day when the retreat turns suddenly into a rout, the vernal equinox, happiest time of all the year, when the day equals the night and you know that you have burst clear out of the long dark pass into the plain of spring.

This we celebrate today, the certain promise of summer springing in the veins of the world.

I have always found it difficult to imagine Christmas in Australia or Tahiti or the Friendly Isles: places where the sun shines hot and the days are long. No doubt Christians have Christmas wherever it finds them. But I count myself lucky to live in the Northern Hemisphere where the mystery of Christmas happens to coincide, more or less exactly, with the older magic of the shortest day. The one reinforces the other. Christian or pagan man, you feel the world turning and the heart lifting.

Meanwhile, work goes on. There are birds to fatten and birds to kill. You never hear of the secret and unacknowledged sadness of those who rear birds. In the moment of culmination and reward there is an admixture of regret which profit does not quite assuage. This is true, I think, in a minor degree, even of the turkey breeder and the poultry farmer, but it is trebly true of the gamekeeper. Fowls and turkeys are perhaps the least amiable of domestic creatures, but nobody can raise game birds who does not in some degree love them. Hence the gamekeeper's mild case of schizophrenia.

Sometimes in summer I fish for carp in a small and secret lake, enclosed by trees. The keeper's cottage stands in a tiny clearing at the water's edge, a most desirable situation, and here too at his door is the mallard nursery. In addition to his pheasants, keeper has been raising wildfowl here for several years; a bold and costly experiment; you do not often find wildfowling so far from the sea. We must be all of forty miles inland. It's a handy distance.

There are kingfishers living nearby – once one lighted on the tip of my rod, the greatest catch. No one has ever believed me, but I grow indifferent to the scepticism of townspeople. A green woodpecker and a pair of pied wagtails and many tits and finches live here; but I sometimes think there is no bird lovelier than the mallard duck. All wildfowl are beautiful, and when you have reared them by hand, guarding them day and night against their innumerable enemies, you do not submit them lightheartedly to the guns of strangers who never saw them before the moment when they flew over, anonymous and unsuspecting.

Sometimes when I am sitting in my secret hide among tall rushes and overhanging boughs, silent as a sentry and relishing the silence like wine, the keeper's door opens across the far side of the pool, a great flash of light. I hear his dog speak once, and the human voice answers, both carrying big and flat across the water. Then I hear nothing more but the small voices of night until the keeper materializes out of the darkness by my side.

Keepers and carp fishers learn to move softly; my friend was a dab hand at unarmed combat, in the days when we both wore the commando flash. He stays to have a smoke and we talk in low voices; sitting there with the reel line crooked over a finger, I hear his heart. He is a proud craftsman; he likes to put up a good show of birds for his master's friends to shoot, or shoot *at*. But he grows attached to his birds. Luckily, the majority of the sportsmen are poor shots; a high survival rate does something to resolve his dilemma.

In winter I miss the midnight carp fishing, which made such a change from television, but now the pike are well on the move, and spinning is a craft, almost an art, some say, scarcely less satisfactory than fishing the subtle fly. And healthy! When you have fished a spinning lure down every lay-by and eddy of a mile or so of river, doing it properly and carefully, keeping your optimism up and your spinner down, then you are ready for a flask of onion soup and bread and meat, or cheese.

I discovered the virtue of the flask of hot onion soup rather late in life, and it instantly did my fishing a power of good. We used to take along a bottle of rough, cheap red wine, and it was quite warming, and exhilarating; but you need obedient fingers to govern a free-running reel, an Ariel or a multiplier; my casts used to get more and more adventurous in the afternoon and I lost a lot of tackle in trees, not to mention the nuisance, on a cold day, of unpicking a 'bird's nest' when the reel developed an overrun.

There is fishing all the year round for those who want it, and I'm not sure that I have not enjoyed the winter spinning as much or almost as much as April's marvellous renewal of trouting. And there are flies to be tied in winter by lamplight. You can't read and tie flies at the same time, but sometimes I'll persuade my wife to read aloud to me from Eric Parker's anthology, *An Angler's Garland,* or from some such untiring masterpiece as Jack Hughes-Parry's *Fishing Fantasy,* or V. Fox-Strangway's curiously neglected *Wandering Fisherman,* which sets your feet itching, or from one of the finest and loveliest fishing books of all, George Brennand's classic *Halcyon,* which I'm glad to see has been reissued; a rare triumph for an angling author, but well deserved.

Of course, with Christmas coming there is a lot to do in the short day besides fishing or thinking about fishing. Kindling has to be cut and cut in plenty, and logs looked after. If I were a truly prudent or thrifty man I should have the winter's supply cut and stacked by autumn, but I don't have the great gift of organization, nor an iron will, and I find myself at the sawbench in mid-winter oftener than becomes a thrifty peasant. Apple wood makes the most fragrant logs, I fancy; beech and birch are fine for merry vigour and sparkle; oak only for a snoozer's stoke-up. 'Slow old oak,' says Alf Norman the forester, who never thinks of himself as a landscape artist, though he is one. Hazel makes good kindling and it satisfies a frugal instinct, for we use up the pea sticks and bean poles from the vegetable plot. Pea sticks must be new each spring: 'Peas won't grow on old wood,' they say. I shall never find out if it is true, for I enjoy too much cutting the new sticks and pressing them into the rich black loam.

The garden changes its aspect completely with the rising of the pea sticks and bean poles. Summer's come, ripeness and maturity seem suddenly at hand. Whatever the weather, you feel that nothing is beyond you, that the earth is inexhaustible, fecund and springing. Bean poles last two seasons or three; it depends how wet the season is. Then they go for firewood. There aren't very many occupations for an idle hour more satisfying than to slice short lengths of superannuated bean pole into thin slivers of kindling, with a murderous great fagging hook. You get over-ambitious, from time to time, and slice off a thin sliver of finger.

Altogether it is a great time of year in the country, and Christmas coming caps all. For weeks past we have been having those high, pearly skies which I think are the loveliest of all, real open weather, wonderful for farmer and fisherman alike. True, the rivers are running down now, strangely low and clear for the time of year, and you have to keep your distance and fish fine and far off. But that will soon be put right, no doubt about it.

You never need worry about the weather in this loveliest of all climates. It always corrects itself nicely and the balance is just right. You can see that from the landscape, not to mention the fine cars which farmers drive to market. God's greatest gift to temperate men is a temperate climate. There is an extra chore to be done in Christmas week and that is to bait up a couple of swims for the Boxing Day fishing. We do two of them with a nice mash of brewer's grains and bran and middlings, with a bit of sharps thrown in and some mashed potatoes and stale bread, kneaded into lumps with a few lob worms and brandlings and gentles pressed into them, for the protein. One baited swim in the river, one in the lake, just to be on the safe side. If the river is in flood we fish the lake, but if the river is in order it is to be preferred, if only because it is traditional.

After the thanksgiving and adoration of Christmas Day, which always cuts to the heart in the country even sharper and keener than ever it did in town, there are few pleasanter ways back to the beauty of everyday life than the long-corking expeditions on Boxing Day. The river is beautifully clear of weeds and you can send your float trotting down the stream, brave and gay, for forty yards and more. I always get a new float as a present, every Christmas, whatever else; a big one that I can see forty yards away. If there is no wind, I glue a little paper pennant to the tip of the quill. The secular ritual of Boxing Day is to return home with a brace of grayling or perch, which are just as sweet as trout, especially if you cook them in bacon fat.

Sometimes, of course, we draw blank, but nothing has the power to diminish the joy of the first fishing trip after the solstice, on the right side of the year. As we come back along the lane, a little weary and maybe cold or wet, there is a beckoning light in the cottage window, and tea a-brewing.

*   *   *   *

Winter

An Indian, wearing a lemon-coloured turban, opened our gate.
Kay sent me to the door to deal with him. I was nothing loth.
Several Indian pedlars had been seen around the village lately,
though they had not called on us, and somehow they had got
rather a bad name. This was not long after we moved from
London to the cottage, and a very long time before 'race' had
become some sort of issue: even so, I was aware that prejudice
existed. The villagers, who were an only moderately gay and
charming bunch, taken all round, had a down on these Indian
pedlars, for reasons which I never elicited. Several had been
advised to get stuffed, and at least one irate cottager had offered
to stuff one princely pedlar's turban down his throat or up his
jacksie, just as he preferred. But the more usual reaction was a
sly closing of the door followed by muttered imprecations on
both sides. I had heard all about this and was rather keen to
meet one of the visitants face to face. I didn't at all mind being
interrupted at my work. I was stuck, and quite certain that I
should never write another line, anyway. It's a feeling you
get.

In Hampstead, where we lived among the nobs before coming
down in the world to the status of cottager, a turbaned Indian
carrying a suitcase looked a perfectly natural part of the scenery.
In the village, I must admit, he looked a shade incongruous,
floating silently through the dimmity, turban gleaming between
the hedgerows.

This Indian caller of ours, who was as handsome as a panto-
mime prince, could scarcely conceal his disappointment when
I appeared at the door, instead of the pretty young housewife.
But he bravely said I was in for a lucky year. I replied that I
hoped he was, too. This may have been a mistake, for he seemed
to brighten up. He offered to tell me my luck if I would fetch
a pencil and a bit of paper. Kay gave me a look of disgust when I
went to fetch them; but I wanted to know my luck. Who
doesn't?

A Cottage Idyll

The prince asked me to tell him my initial, and whether or not I had any children. I answered truthfully. He wrote something in one corner of the paper, tore it off, folded it very small, put it in the palm of my hand and closed my fingers over it.

He then asked me to name a number below five. I said four. On the paper which he had retained he wrote 3 2. Then he asked me to cross out one of those figures. I crossed out the 3. He wrote 3, and drew a circle round it.

He then asked me what was my favourite flower. I said 'rose', and he wrote it down. So on the paper was written ROSE 3.

'Now look at the other paper,' the prince commanded.

I unscrewed the scrap of paper which had been clenched in my fist all this time. On it was written ROSE 3.

I don't know what it proves.

The prince seemed slightly annoyed to learn that other Indians had been before him. We had a cup of tea together and exchanged many wild highflown statements and courteous assertions, and eventually he took his leave, drifting down the lane like an exotic flower in the dusk. I hadn't bought any of his rubbish but I'm ashamed to admit that I had given him a very small sum of money, much smaller than he liked but much more than I really wished to give. Neither of us came out of the operation just as we might have hoped, but on the other hand we operated as human beings, with all that that implies . . .

The rustic screen which I so laboriously built was already earning its keep. If it had not been there the Indian prince would undoubtedly have come straight to the inconvenient door which leads directly into our living room. Everybody used to. Intimidated by this vast maze of boughs which I erected, he automatically went round to the other side of the cottage, to the official 'front' door, which leads only into an easily defensible little maze of porches, passages, halls and cubby-holes and other doors, all about five feet high. This way into the cottage is fraught with peril for the stranger. Sometimes new visitors go off in search of the cloakroom and are rescued, much later, miserably looking at the pictures in my study. Doubly lost.

I did not have the brass neck to make the rustic screen on site, open to the censure of every expert passer-by. So I built it on the back lawn, secretly, and solidly. I was delighted with it when it was done, but unfortunately it proved infinitely too heavy for me to lift.

I had to suborn Alan, our sturdy farming friend, to help me heave it off the ground, and we staggered round the house like a couple of property men shifting scenery for *The Petrified Forest*. We then had to dig a series of post-holes to take the massive main uprights. Post-hole digging is a craft all to itself, infinitely laborious, and calling not only for strength and endurance but for a certain cunning. Anyone can dig a hole, given time, but a small, deep hole which stays parallel instead of growing ever wider at the top, that is another thing again. I must confess that Alan dug some seventy per cent of the holes. He also rather ostentatiously took out his knife and cleaned my spade. I hope I can take a hint.

Anyway, the rustic screen survives, and has survived these many years; one of my rather few material memorials. It was rapidly grown over by climbing roses: we used 'Paul's Scarlet Climber', 'Emily Gray', 'Excelsa', and Easlea's 'Golden Rambler'. They all seemed quite happy, though these yellow and creamy roses are never quite so satisfactory, in my opinion: they start with a gallant rush but tend to flop off a bit. Still, it was soon quite a jolly sight, a sort of extension to our front wall, and it made the side garden private to some extent, and diverted guests, both wanted and unwanted, round to the other side of the house, where they could be ensnared, encouraged, discouraged, or in any other way that seemed appropriate, handled.

I wouldn't wish you to think that we were unduly cagey about visitors. On the contrary, I could hardly be interrupted too often, having a great weakness for knocking-off for a little rest and break, and though Kay was always a shade more circumspect than me, in fact greatly more circumspect, we enjoyed entertaining our callers, by and large. Neither of us really belongs to that category of chatterers who are always telling anybody who will listen, on television and off, 'I love *people*,' as if that undiscriminating remark somehow places them firmly on the side of the angels. I love some people, some of the time. On the other hand, we are not misanthropes. You remember that couple in Conan Doyle's novel, *The Mystery of Cloober*, one of his early ones, who stuck up a sign by their gate reading: 'General and Mrs Heatherstone have no wish to increase the circle of their acquaintance.' Great stuff, if you can find it in you. No, we were not on that level. But I can understand people who enjoy their own company best. Not far from us there lives a scholarly old lady who spends most of her time working away at a mass of forbiddingly official-looking documents and books, White Papers, Blue Books, I don't know what. You can see her at it at her study window every time you pass. I always give her a cheery wave but it is never returned. She had a nice old raggedly orchard alongside her shack, much coveted by goddam property speculators and that sort of swine. One day she must have slipped out very early – you almost never see her out, though she is known to feed the birds every dawn – and we had the joy of reading this notice, pinned on her gate:

> Miss Smith wishes it to be known that she does not intend to sell her plot. She is quite well. She does not wish to be interrupted.

It takes pluck to do a thing like that. Character. Personally I rather welcome the knock at the door, but it takes all sorts, and most of them are incapable of assimilating the simple fact that a writer is a worker like any other worker. They mostly seem to believe that writing is something you just knock off betweentimes, like dashing off a letter. I'm not asking for sympathy, I've got the life I wanted, but a writer has working hours like any other toiler, with this difference, that there is no union official or foreman to tell him when to knock off.

*   *   *   *

Alf Norman the forester had a fine fire going in the clearing by his hut. On this wind, a cool one from the North, woodsmoke drifts across to us in fitful aromatic gusts. In between the pungent gouts of woodsmoke you can smell Alf's pipe, and when you get round to windward you can catch the strange faint aroma of rotting leaves.

This reminds me that we are always going to build a lean-to and spreader of oak staves, so that we can smoke the fish we catch, the trout and salmon especially, and maybe some eels and sea fish, over a surly slow smouldering of oak shavings.

But that is one of the things that may never get done. We catch so few fish these days. The hunting spirit has been largely exorcised. It comes and goes like the wind. I fished at every opportunity for about forty years, from six to forty-six, then I gave it up. But it wouldn't stay given-up. You cannot mess about so arbitrarily with the deeper desires of your soul. I am still almost a non-angler, in the sense that I don't practise the sport much, but it is always welling up inside me, the old urge to be at the waterside, and sometimes I give way to it. Nowadays I fish exclusively 'for the pot': somehow that makes it respectable. I have almost given up the coarse fisher's pursuit, apart from the ritual Boxing Day outing and some pike fishing and perch fishing, for I can no longer permit myself to hook fish simply for fun, fish to be unhooked and returned to the water 'uninjured', as they say, which means only slightly injured. But since I eat a lot of fish, I see no sin in catching and killing the fish I eat. If anything, it is a bit less cruel than buying fish from the fish-monger. At least I know that my fish die swiftly, one bang on the head and it is all over. The ethics of what we eat are involved and

57

tortuous. One thing only is certain: you cannot live on air, you can live only by the death of other organisms. The act of killing grows distasteful, but that may be a sign of over-civilization. So I can still persuade myself to catch and kill the strong-hearted food fish – themselves all predators, vigorous killers: the powerful bass, trout, salmon, grayling, the flounders, soles and plaice, skate and eels, pike and perch and the delicious gudgeon, mackerel and huss. And catching them is still – except for the inevitable moments of death when I feel the iron entering my own soul, a foretaste of my own death – it is still a pursuit that absorbs and engrosses, a time-annihilator, a capsule in which one escapes the gravitational pull of worldly time and trifles.

Too weak to kill, too weak to live. Too sensitive to death, too sensitive for life. Yet we are what we are, and that is changeless. Or does the evolutionary process go a tiny bit further in one life and lifetime? Can we end a shade higher up the ladder than we began?

It must be so, or there could be no evolution at all. Progress must have a time-scale and it must be divisible into individual life spans; measurable in minutes. There must be moments of perception and change. Can we learn to die wiser than we are born? Not merely more knowledgeable, which is automatic even in the most foolish, but more innocent? Newborn we are not innocent, but ignorant. To survive knowledge and acquire wisdom ... Just one tiny fraction of the possible perception ... To reject the principle of aggrandisement and learn to love ...

> Territory, status, and love, sing all the birds,
> are what matters ...

I have never brought myself to shoot the birds. I love guns, which have a hard beauty of their own, but I love birds more. Yet they are combative and intransigent. The robins have marked out their winter territory and are always ready to defend it, against real or imagined aggression, with a furious obstinacy that is almost human. The hedge sparrows have made it plain which lengths of hedgerow they regard as their own, and the coal tits are raiding the milk bottles almost before the milkman (who wears a bowler hat and a long plastic mac) has turned his back.

I don't honestly know what life offers that is lovelier than a flight of wild duck, seen against a pearly winter sky. With blue mist mantling the distant ridge of downs, and a lighted window at the end of the lane.

My friend Hugh Falkus shoots wild duck. I think he would almost rather go duck shooting than anything: though one should not speak for another's wishes. Hugh is a great character, a large person, larger than life as it is lived in these emaciated times of too much mass communication and too little private communication. He has had a strange, chequered life, full of drama and not without tragedy: he is a brave man. He is very big and handsome and a great fighter, but as gentle as need be. Hugh lives in a remote cottage near the coast of Cumberland, with his own stretch of sea trout fishing, and bass to be had in plenty a little further out when the sea trout have departed the estuary. But above all else, as I said, he loves wildfowling. It is strange how wildfowling attracts men of marked individuality and (sometimes, not always) poetic sensibility. You have to be out of the rut of commonplaces to fancy this rare, weird game of wildfowling, lying out on marshes and saltings, struggling through mud and across treacherous pills and creeks, crouching for hours in hides or lying motionless in a punt, in the bitter weather of a wintry dawn. It is the wildest, most romantical of sports surviving to us.

To me the mallard, widgeon, teal and geese are too lovely to be shot: but I eat them with relish when they are given to me, already irrevocably dead. It is the coward's part. Some of my friends are wildfowlers: they have more resolution and are not so troubled by weaknesses of the imagination and sensibility. Yet we are all murderers *manqués*. Or almost all. But the trend of the times is all towards a new hypocrisy. Young housewives abound who don't know the first thing about buying meat. Butchers secretly despise them, and kindle to an old hand who knows what she is buying, and why. I see the girl-wives in the big stores and supermarkets, contentedly buying bloodless cuts wrapped hygienically in plastic: they take what is there, ignorant and apathetic. Or they buy from the deep-freeze. It is the new hypocrisy: everything served up in a neat, trim, bloodless packaging, as far removed as possible from the living, natural, bloody reality, the reality of farmyard and field, garden and stockyard and coppice. And all the year round everything is 'in season'. So we lose track of the seasons. We get out of step with nature's rhythm. We are living an unreal life. It is the first time in history that man has been able to ignore the natural rhythm in this way; and this is only the beginning. Soon we shall be eating synthetic proteins. I don't say this is wholly bad; it is probably inevitable, anyway. But it isn't the texture of life as we used to live it. Something of the nature goes out of life when you get so clever, so synthetic. It is reflected in the emotional life, of course. Nature is our only true touchstone.

To get back to 'our' mallard, and the humour and irony of life ... There is one recurring situation which catches them out in a rather amusing way.

Where rain lies on a field of winter corn it catches the pale gleam of the sun, sneaking out to shine for a little while before it sets behind the blue-grey hills. The heavy soil holds the water for a time, and it glitters like a lake. This puzzles the mallard community that live on the real lake nearby.

The mallard are continually taking off and skimming the tops of the tall trees that stand sentinel in a magic ring around their secret home. Then they circle the false lake, that has appeared so mysteriously. They dip and swoop and sometimes it looks as if they are going to land on the green corn, a couple of inches tall,

Winter

that is just barely covered by the water. But they never do. At the last moment they spot the deception and wheel up exquisitely against the evening sky. Crying and speculating they fly back home. Over the tall trees with inches to spare, then down in a steep dive, to land on the lake with a crash that reverberates among the bare trunks.

* * * *

They say it is 'as bright as day' under the full moon, but of course it is as different from daylight as candlelight is from gas. As we draw the curtains the moon comes up like a vast Cheshire cheese behind the farmhouse over the way from Tea-Cosy Cottage. Next time you chance a look, the bare elms standing against a deep blue sky dominate and enclose your world.

The first full moon of the first New Year after we moved in was just about as beautiful as anything I remember. Perhaps it was partly because strong cold winds had swept the sky clean. Day after day started dirty, with clinging mist or charcoal-coloured clouds. Then after lunch a wind got up and pushed the clouds about the sky and finally swept them out of sight, and sunset after sunset was painfully magnificent. It is when such a wind is at work that you see the real cerulean, the 'heavenly blue'. It's a misty old island most of the time, even on comparatively clear days: you only get the glittering, vivid 'Greek light' after a few days of hard northerly or north-easterly winds. It's like the day you first get glasses.

This is the time when you really see the extreme greenness of the countryside in mid-winter. Even at night, under such a sky and with a great moon like this, you can see the rose-red wall of the cottage flushing a pale faint pink, and the emerald and viridian streaks of lichen on the boles of trees stand out quite vividly.

But beautiful as the nights have been, it is in daytime that you spot the first signs of the 'turn of the year'. One solitary snowdrop was out under the weeping cherry in the middle of the back lawn on the seventh of January, the earliest I remember. It was quickly followed by whole clumps of them under the holly by the porch. Primulas are in flower, too, on the mossy bank, but the aconites which usually lead the year's proud procession are later this time.

This is my sort of gardening. Put the bulbs in and let them 'naturalize' themselves. It's wonderful to see them multiply. I must say I'm not really a gardener, though Kay is quite expert, keen and diligent, and scholarly. I like the wild stuff best. Perhaps it is mere laziness.

But aconites were out in time – they always are – to meet winter's last desperate dying kick. Sacrificial outriders of spring, snowdrops and aconites live their lives in a bitter season and reaffirm the luxuriant hope of less temerarious organisms. To see them, I have heard say, is to believe.

We expected hard weather when the gulls flew inland over forty miles of ridge and valley and settled screaming on the broad pasture. We knew it again when the hoodlum crows, those furtive gangsters of the lower air, began to muscle in on the breakfast which we put out for friendlier and more domesticated birds.

The first tentative drifts of snowflakes came low and slow, wandering, almost horizontally, on variable airs, and falling at length unmarked on the frozen ground. The cows didn't know which way to turn. They like to present their rumps to the wind. But the wind shifts and swings between north and east, and eddies madly off the shoulder of the downs. All over the meadow cows are facing in different directions, puzzled and disunited. Cowmen will confirm that there is usually a leader cow which the others follow, but this wind ruins leadership.

Those crows are low-bred, shabby creatures, but their relatives the jackdaws are amusing. All birds come nearer to the house when the weather hardens, the little ones brisk and perky and knowing, and even in their unrelenting pugnacity delightful to watch. But the big black brethren circle warily in leaning sweeps, an ancestry of furtive theft implicit in that sidelong swooping approach. When one summons the resolution to land, he is on his toes, trembling with fear, and away again in an instant, often without the morsel he landed for. But if he masters the moment and starts to peck, he stuffs his beak with five or six mouthfuls before flapping away again. Much the same is true of the beautiful, piratical jays.

Now again the wind has shifted and the snow holds off. It is a battle in the air between the stealthy, infiltrating Siberian freeze and the roistering tempest from the north. Our hopes are with the north. If winter must stage one last demonstration of its spite, then the open attack with buffets and trumpets, mounted by wild island-bearing seas, is more bearable than the silent, life-hating freeze that steals in from Siberia. God preserve us from endless inland plains. Great land masses with their arid extremes of heat and cold breed arid and extreme fanaticism. Mind and spirit reel in their parched monotony. Moscow, five degrees, and dry: Delhi, 105 degrees, and dry. Equally unattractive. All civilization is coastal. Our island is little more than a rock wet with sea spray. Nowhere a hundred miles distant, the moderating sea anneals the brittle human temper and makes it flexible and tolerant.

*   *   *   *

The mocking sunshine makes this frozen world look beautiful. Before the sun came out it looked bedraggled and uncomely as a farmyard.

The sun is shining on the bare elms and the ancient withy tree across the road and you can suddenly see every crevice and canyon of the bark. I am waiting for the brilliant flash of Yaffle, the great green woodpecker, who occasionally appears from nowhere in his prince's plumage and investigates the corrugated bark with his battering beak.

A Cottage Idyll

On the north side, the bark is elephant grey like that of other old trees anywhere. But on the south side it is vivid with lichen. It is hard to believe that the smooth matt coat of lichen, like a coat of sprayed green paint, is in fact a swarming colony of living organisms.

Between us and the sun stand flowering-currant bushes which we planted near the gate. They are so far ahead now that their wine-red elongated buds glow translucent like stained glass. And the smooth tawny skin of the young willow trees flushes in the sunlight to the delicate heady hue of Rhine wines. All these signs come in an afternoon to give you reassurance. Then the sun is hidden again and seal-dark snow clouds challenge you to find them beautiful.

It will soon be time to push off outdoors and make the rounds of the fuel stores. Stoking up against nightfall is a chore that suddenly assumes urgent importance when a cold snap comes. It is surprising how much time and energy these basic chores consume. If you fret about it, you are lost, in the wrong life. You have to accept it all as part of a slow but satisfying rhythm. Humping in coal and oil, logs and kindling is a pleasant routine occupation. You don't have to think of it as 'eating into your time' – it *is* your time, it is one of the life's profound little pleasures and satisfactions. If you feel otherwise, if it irks you and you grow impatient to be done with it and back at something else, then you are in the wrong groove.

What happens to all that time when summer comes and the re-fuelling chore does not have to be done? I do not know the answer.

I'm afraid that I am a procrastinator by nature. Reluctant to plan ahead, I do my best work at the last moment, against the clock. That is the pattern of my professional life, the result of having to meet deadlines all my days. The habit leaks over into these very unprofessional chores.

In December, when it gets dark at 4 p.m., I am moving like a shadow at 3.55 p.m., with hod and scuttle and oil drum. When it gets dark at 6, I am on my rounds at 5.55. I am always promising myself to get ahead, but I enjoy it all so much, I know I shall never change.

We tell each other, this must be winter's last spiteful fling. Soon will come generous days when you don't have to seek to find the beauty of the world, it hits you in the eye. Meanwhile the winter routine of morning and evening persists for a little longer. Breakfast for the trusting birds who gather at first light near the kitchen door. Fuel for the human hearth when the light fails. In between these acts of mercy and prudence the day is short. But each is longer than the last.

Sometimes when you are walking down the lane, leaning against a bitter wind, you become aware that birds are singing, beautifully. You stop, surprised, and peer around the bare trees trying to spot the singer; and sometimes the singer sings unseen.

It is strange to hear wild birds singing now, in the starving weather. What have they to sing about? But that is one of the mysteries of song and spirit. What had poor consumptive Keats to sing about? The mystery and marvel of song is that it comes when it comes, unplanned and unsolicited. No dictator can order music to spring from the air. At one moment it has no existence. Then it is born in the mind of the creator. And once it appears, and is remembered, it is a victory for ever over the unruly forces of oblivion, the dark undifferentiated mass of time.

We pare fat off our meat ration and chop it small for the singing birds. And for the songless, too. There is no means test and no music test. No bird has to sing for its supper. I carry it out, with the daily bread, to the bird table in the garden, and all the way I am aware that unseen eyes are watching me.

I have not moved five paces from the bird table before they are swooping on it. It is a curious thing, one of the many little mysteries, best unexplained, which give life some of its richness, that I made that bird table rather nicely, right first time, without any hitches or afterthoughts, and in about thirty minutes flat. Yet when I make something for myself I have to concentrate quite grimly all the time, I cut myself, I spoil good timber. It's a battle all the way. I get it about right, but it is all work – working against the grain of my tiny talent.

For the birds it went right.

I do not pretend to understand this. It makes me feel slightly superstitious. But perhaps all work that is done with love goes well?

My loftier friends, those better equipped with brains, are uneasy in the presence of those words, love, and luck. But I cannot help believing in them. Or, to put it another way, perhaps a more accurate way: I cannot imagine life without love and luck. I don't want to imagine it.

*   *   *   *

We had the greatest luck in finding Lily. Through our married life we have had long spells of coping by ourselves, and intervals of domestic help. One of these intervals lasted about ten years, and in many ways it was the happiest time of our lives, and it was all due to Lily. In our minds Lily and Tea-Cosy Cottage are inextricably linked. There have been other cottages and other helpers but it is Tea-Cosy Cottage and Lily, fused together in memory, which shall never be forgotten.

Things have changed in the village now, but when we went to live there we were the first invaders, the only strangers, the only household that was not in some way tied, economically, to the activities of the village and its farms. In those days there were women who were actually quite eager to do some part-time domestic work, and men who were actually keen to do some spare-time gardening. We actually had a choice. We were beset by volunteers.

And very lucky. We chose Lily to give a hand in the house and

Alan to give a hand in the garden. Both turned out to be characters of the unforgettable kind.

Lily lived in the cottage next door, with her sister Margaret. Two spinsters who loved cats and gardening and were soaked in the history of the village. Margaret went out to work in the nearby town, Lily stayed at home and kept house. And it gave her actual pleasure to come in and do some housework for us. Though not, perhaps, so much pleasure as it gave us. The whole history of domestic labour is fraught with sadness and misunderstanding, and I don't wonder that it is almost all in the past now, that 'servants' appear only in the homes of the very rich. And then are largely foreign. The British do not relish being anybody's servants, and some of us do not relish being anybody's masters. The new emancipation, which was only really completed by the Second World War, though it began with the First, is absolutely right and understandable. Yet there was another side to the relationship, a happier side. In some homes, as I know for sure from personal observation and from others' accounts, there was a genuinely happy and self-respecting relationship of trust and affection between the two sides. In fact they were not two sides, but one circle. In those rare cases – were they really so rare? I don't know – when the 'servants' and their bosses felt that they were genuinely all members of one family, a household with specialized functions but one common objective, then self-respect and affection and trust could really flourish, there was no trace of envy or bossiness or any of the horrid social nuances which poison life. And some trace of all this, this happier relationship, survived in our life with Lily.

Lily had been put 'to service' as soon as she left school, at the age of fourteen. Her first situation was at Drungewick Manor in Sussex, a great black-and-white Elizabethan house later owned by the theatrical impresario, Gilbert Miller. So she knew domestic service from the bottom up; you might say she was conditioned to servility. But you might be wrong. Lily had a natural courtesy born and bred in her, yes: she insisted on calling me Sir and Kay Madam, and nothing we could do would dissuade her from using those archaic terms. But I hope and believe that I'm right in saying that our courtesy was equal to hers: the relationship between us was one of genuine human dignity, mutual respect, and after a very short time, real affection. We became friends, and we remain friends to this day, though nowadays Lily and Meg live in a bungalow in another village and Kay and I live in a bungalow in yet another. Time's whirligig hath made bungalow-dwellers of us all.

Lily had nominal mornings 'on', three a week, but in fact we were in and out of each other's cottages all the time. Cats were a great bond; gardening another. Our cat at the time was the notorious Badger, later to be succeeded by the devilish twins, Casey and Brady. (See my little book *Life with Badger*, published by John Baker.) Lily's cats were Tommy and Nigger, and it is hard to say which household pampered its cats more. We were bad enough, but Lily perhaps had the edge on us. Certainly Badger immediately recognized a cat-spoiler extraordinary, and became devoted to Lily, who spoiled him, in our absences, which in those days were quite frequent, to such an extent that we invariably returned to an animal who practically refused to acknowledge our existence.

Lily had been a beautiful girl and was still an extraordinarily handsome woman, with very fine eyes, the sight of which, alas, was already threatened. She had relatives all over the village and its neighbouring hamlets, and marked our card authoritatively on the little ways of our neighbours. But although she had her share of normal human prejudices, as we all have, she was apparently without malice. She was also one of nature's born gardeners, a genuine case of green fingers. Her garden was a riot. It was made to no perceptible plan: the only guiding principle seemed to be, 'If there's a square inch of soil vacant, stuff something in'. Everything grew for Lily. Since she filled every square inch with plants, there was no room for weeds. Kay learned a tremendous lot from her.

Indoors, much the same generous and all-accepting principle seemed to be at work. Lily's living room was like her garden: you could just about thread your way through, if you were careful. It was jam-packed with furniture and china ornaments, frankly a bit of a nightmare to me, yet essentially snug and cosy. Lily's energy seemed to be inexhaustible. 'On the go from morning till night,' the old phrase went; and it was literally true of Lily. Of course it is possible to see her as 'under-privileged', scandalously lacking in leisure and opportunity: yet the simple fact is that her life was full and interesting and, so far as human life may be, not unhappy. I do not say this in any spirit of smugness: it is literally true, I think, from my own observation. Life may appear to have endowed Lily on a very grudging scale, and I certainly would not defend the justice of the endowment. But she is one of those people who put into life more than they seek to take out, and for such, it seems, there are never enough hours in the day in which to do interesting things. To put it at the lowest, there is no boredom, apparently no possibility of boredom, in such a life.

Our 'active' association with Lily, or rather hers with us, ran for about a dozen years; though, as I have said, the association in a looser form has always been maintained. By her ready assumption of responsibility she made it possible for us to travel, in those days when we still enjoyed travelling, without the slightest doubt or remorse or backward look towards the cottage and its feline gods. This is a debt which we are unable to repay.

Our gardener was the second Alan in our lives. There was Alan the farmer and there was Alan the farm worker. We were on good terms with both, and from both received endless instruction in country ways, as well as certain insights into country thinking which may have been involuntary. Alan the gardener was an essentially sweet and simple character. He expected rather little from life, and needless to say his wish was granted. He raised a large sturdy family, he and his redoubtable wife: children whom we have watched grow up, children of exceptional energy and spriteliness and indomitable optimism. They have all done well for themselves, as the saying goes. Alan has taken to Christianity in later life, taken to it avidly, I hear, and I have no doubt that its exemplary morality suits his nature very well. But at the time when we knew him he was unconverted, and though sunny and generous to a fault, he had the gift of strong language to a degree which he himself seemed unaware of. Virtually every sentence was larded with 'bloody'. Needless to say this gave no offence to me: my own tendency is along the same lines, I fear. But Kay shuddered a little, from time to time. However, the manner in which Alan swore was somehow disarming: you became aware, very soon, that he used the words without even hearing them, they were a natural part of the vocabulary with which he had grown up. Still, it made a change, after the punctilio of our previous life, to carry on a conversation at the kitchen door with this sweet-natured man:

' 'Evening, Mrs Wiggin. Bloody cold again.'

'It *is* rather cold, Alan. And how's the family?'

'Not so bloody bad, thank you. Shall I weed the bloody rose plot first, or would you like me to get on with earthing up the 'taters? That bloody blight's at 'em again.'

Alan fought a total war against the gardener's innumerable foes. He never relaxed. For him the garden was a battlefield and a whole justification. I could never see it so myself, but came eventually to see his ceaseless endeavours in an almost epic light. Yet he loved the occupation. He was not content with tending his own garden, and ours, and one or two others from time to time. He also laboured on a large allotment near the churchyard, the grass of which he also cut in his spare-time. I have seen him working his allotment, digging away, by the light of the full moon, many and many a time. Here he raised magnificent vegetables. Like most country gardeners, his heart was in vegetable growing. Kay's was in flowers, and, increasingly as time wore on, in shrubs. We have now almost reached a point at which we would even (almost) dispose of the roses, apart from the odd creepers and climbers, and specialize in shrubs. But in the Tea-Cosy Cottage days, we grew a nice mixture, all the vegetables we needed and far more, all our salad stuffs, far too much fruit, a lot of flowers, a lot of roses and a few shrubs. And a damn sight too much grass, it goes without saying. I used to share the common delusion that 'putting it down to grass' was a labour-saving move, but of course it is not. Grass is real hard work; endlessly demanding and not entirely rewarding. Monotonous.

Alan is the only man I have ever known who reduced his own rate of pay out of a delicate awareness of the employer's financial plight. For this gesture, alone, he will be greeted warmly by the custodian of the pearly gates, when his time comes. At the beginning we settled on a rate of three shillings an hour. After a few months, Alan one evening hemmed and haw'd a bit while lighting his pipe at the kitchen door, before departing into the blackening dusk. Eventually he got it out.

'I don't want three shillings an hour any more. I'll take half a crown.'

'Why is that, Alan?'

'I don't think you can afford it.'

Now isn't that a wonderful thing to hear? It was true that I couldn't afford it, but I insisted on paying it. The man spoke from his heart, a simple observation based on insight and natural goodness. No messing, no beating about the bush. That is the attitude of a man who does not see life entirely in terms of grab and get. You can imagine we cherished him. I hope that we made it up to him, in some measure, before the day came when we had to part.

Alan was the best hand with a scythe that I ever knew. I

bought a scythe at his instigation, for keeping down the grass in the orchard. It was wonderful to watch him sharpening it. Even then, only yesterday, so to speak, in the nineteen-fifties, there were very few men who could swing a scythe, and fewer who could sharpen one. I learned from Alan how to do it, but never acquired his ease and rhythm. He was also a dab hand with the fagging hook, or semi-sickle, an instrument which not everyone can master. He could cut round a sapling growth in perfect security – even Henry Williamson's little oak, a gift from his coppice at Ox's Cross in Devon, survived close trimming all round.

Alan and his family, and Lily too, maintained their belief in country remedies long after mass-communications had spread popular hypochondria far and wide among the populace. Since my own mother was a great believer in all sorts of simples – we were regularly drenched with things like yarrow tea, wormwood, camomile, liquorice root – this came quite naturally. We didn't actually use the remedies ourselves, though. Kay reminded me one evening, after we had had a learned discourse from Alan on the curative properties of something or other, I fancy it was dandelions, about the ointment put up by old Adams, the cemetery keeper of our native village of Bloxwich in Staffordshire. It was black, pungent, and glutinous, and was widely held to be equally efficacious for piles, ringworm, bunions, bronchitis and belly-ache. There was a local Black Country joke about old Adams's ointment which may well illustrate our native wit. 'If you stuck it on the wall of the bank it'd draw your money out,' they used to say. Dark and various were the speculations about its ingredients. Mr Adam's occupation, at the cemetery, naturally gave rise to some ingenious theories.

*   *   *   *

Before the rain came birds were having dust baths in the rose plots and flower beds. As soon as the night frost eased away and the fine top-soil was bone dry again, legions of little birds squatted down in the sunshine, wriggling their small bodies and fluffling out their feathers. Wherever a bird took a dust bath there was a little hollow, scooped out as neatly as if you had taken a small pudding basin and pressed it into the soil.

I don't know whether the dust baths gave them dry throats, or whether it was a simple question of the prevailing dryness of the atmosphere, but during the dust bath spell there was a steady progress or procession of visitors to the drinking water. To some eyes a man taking a drink is a comical sight, but a bird taking a drink is even odder. It looks for all the world as if the bird is gargling.

The bird opens its beak and shoves it smartly through the water, scooping up a drop, and then it raises its head almost vertical and lets the water trickle down its throat. It looks as if the bird has no swallowing mechanism and has to rely on gravity. I do not say this is true, but it is how it looks.

Most birds seem to be satisfied with one or at most two dips, scoops and gargles at a time. Starlings seem to take three or four short ones, and sometimes another one for the road; but the only bird that we see really knocking them back is a slender and beautiful thrush. This one is a dipsomaniac.

There is another thrush in the garden, known to us as Old Fatso; doubtless a vulgar name, but irresistible, I'm afraid. This is a steady and slow-thinking bird, so fat it is practically spherical. Most of our local thrushes seem rather nervous of the truculent blackbirds, which are by a wide margin the most pugnacious birds in the garden, I'm sorry to say. But no blackbird gives Old Fatso the rush.

Curiously, Fatso makes no great show in the morning bread-line. He turns up, as a general rule, and accepts the odd crumb; but the whole business is obviously a bit beneath him. He must have private means.

He is a very self-possessed bird. We don't like the greedy

starlings to collar more than their share, and sometimes when the small birds are outnumbered Kay throws open the kitchen casement and remarks in a schoolmarmish voice, 'Rather too many starlings, I think.'

The starlings rise then with a froosh of wings, but Old Fatso takes not the slightest bit of notice. At most, he turns his back on her and toddles slowly away, as if deep in thought.

When the thaw came, of course, the birds were wild with joy. On the first wet morning after the iron sequence of frosts there were worming parties hard at it all over the grass. While they were all so occupied Old Fatso quietly turned up at the kitchen door and tucked in to a private meal of nourishing carbohydrates. He isn't that shape by accident.

*   *   *   *

Nobody who was in the cottage at the time is likely to forget the night the spare bed threw Wally.

This bedstead cost us 19s. 6d. We bought it from the junk shop in the market town because it more or less matched another black enamelled single iron bedstead which we inherited from Kay's ma. Kay went to work on these grim institutional bedsteads and I must say she transformed them. She painted them white and created a chaste effect of restrained luxury by picking out the ornamental bulbous bits in gold.

Our old friend Wally, perhaps our most frequent visitor at the cottage, is a bachelor. He was a bachelor then and is a bachelor now, and, I should guess, incurable. Like most bachelors, he is inclined to coddle himself. On his first visit he fussily tested the mattresses and conducted a finicking close check for draughts; then he adopted one of the beds as his own.

All went well for a year or two, but as time went by my old comrade, once the pride of the barrack square, or at least of the cookhouse and orderly room, began to put on weight. He got up to sixteen stone. Illogically, he developed a parallel tendency to find fault with the bed, which did not keep pace with him. We were almost persuaded that the old bed resented Wally's criticism. It began to play him up.

The wooden floor of the spare room (or, as Kay put it, the guest room) slopes rather dramatically. It is constructed of vast rough beams, with surprising gaps between them, hewn in an age before the machine shop and the square, hewn by eye, and hewn, I often think, by an eye influenced by strong drink. Time and use have polished them to a high gloss. One night, after a big polishing day, Wally's bed began to move under its own power as soon as he got into it.

It crossed the room at increasing speed and fetched up against the far wall with a shock that might have pitched Wally clean through the window had he not been clinging desperately to the bed head, uttering cries of fear.

Wally's suspicions of the bed date from that incident. He wanted to get the hacksaw and whip off the castors there and then, but we calmed him down by agreeing to fit the legs of the bedstead into little glass pots, you know the things I mean. We found a set of four in the junk shop, rather nice greenish glass pots the use of which baffled the shop's owner completely. This helped us to obtain them for a fair price.

Well, the other night Wally toddled off to bed and we sat on by the fire, waiting for him to get through with the bathroom and thinking night thoughts. The first thud did not disturb us. We assumed that Wal had simply forgotten to duck. It was a very bruising complex of old beams. But the thud was followed by a reverberating crash. The din drew me upstairs. I found Wally on his back, half under the bed, fighting to get one leg of the bedstead back into its glass what-not.

It had jumped out as he put his weight on the bed. That was the thud. Wally was caught off balance, the mat slid from under him on the glassy beams, and he went down. That was the crash. The flex of the bedside lamp was twined round his ankle. As he crawled out from under the bed the lamp fell on his head.

By this time Kay was at the bedroom door, seeking enlightenment. I was in no condition to speak, but a voice charged with feeling came out of the darkness.

'It threw me,' said Wally.

*   *   *   *

I watch the riders go by the cottage, at the walk, at the trot, at the canter. And I wonder if the vivid increase in the horse population might yet bring back the fine old trade of horse-manure dealer.

I was never actually in the business, but was what you might call on the fringe of it. It was a highly organized trade when I was a boy. There were always a few do-it-yourself enthusiasts who nipped out with shovel and bucket after a co-operative horse had passed. But these were prim and furtive creatures who tended to look hurriedly to left and right before scurrying back to their compost heaps with their gains. Regular traders despised these dilettanti and never sold them a load, however serious the shortage – and it was getting pretty serious during the Twenties, when I was growing up. They were regarded as being 'black', and I did hear rumours that the odd greenhouse got a brick-end through it, but I never knew the details.

You couldn't consider yourself properly in the business unless you had a little cart made of soap boxes begged from the grocer and mounted on discarded perambulator wheels. That was the basic equipment. For mobility was everything in this heroic trade.

Even at that time, in the Black Country where I was a boy, the motor car had begun to make things difficult for gardeners and allotment holders, and there was a brisk competitive demand for the product. The difficulty was to get at it before your rivals. Organization was the answer. Almost every street had its co-operative, and take-over bids were frequent. In my day the leading groups were the Parker Street Mob, the Bell Lane Dongers, and a crowd from Revival Street who were known, if you please, as the Revivalists. It was a leading Donger who had the brilliant idea of taking the cart with him to afternoon school, so that he could get on the streets ahead of his rivals, who had to run all the way home for theirs. A deeply unimaginative teacher made him leave it outside, tied to the railings, and gave him two with the tawse just to encourage private enterprise.

But the idea paid off, and for some days the Dongers were rolling in the stuff, as you might say.

When the secret got about the Revivalists played a dirty trick. Two of them played the wag one afternoon and pinched the cart from its place by the railings. It was never seen again. Before that row died down fathers and mothers and big brothers and even big sisters had been drawn into it. The fight flared up again at evening surgery, where many were receiving treatment, and several families found themselves short at the end of the week through lost time.

The Parker Street Mob took full advantage of the preoccupation of their rivals, and made what amounted to a corner in the commodity. This led in the nature of things to a sort of armed truce between the Revivalists and the Dongers, who made a treaty setting out strict territorial limits, which were honoured for several days.

It couldn't last, of course. Horses were getting fewer all the time. One heavenly evening I saw the Mob, the Dongers and the Revivalists all bearing down on one inconsiderable harvest, uttering wild cries of rage and defiance. A wheel flew off the Dongers' cart and put them out of the running, but the Mob and the Revivalists met head-on, and the casualties were fearful. I suppose that was the last major engagement, and it marked, more or less, the end of an honourable trade. As one battered Mobster put it, when he called at our kitchen door for a drop of iodine, 'Oss manure ain't worth it. Yo' can mek more scrumpin' opples.'

*   *   *   *

Not being an extra-sensory perceptionist, I did not realize when we took over this blessed plot that we were also taking over the mineral rights to a rich lode of ore which might be known to the more recondite of archaeologists as the Floggit Bequest. The good Floggit was one of my innumerable predecessors at Tea-Cosy Cottage. I never had the joy of knowing him. But even if I hadn't been told, I should have had no difficulty in divining that he carried on here a furtive and squalid business concerning decrepit motor vehicles. For traces of his activities abounded in the soil, as we discovered the moment we began to convert a totally neglected half-acre of weeds into a garden.

I suppose that archaeologists of the future might have worked themselves into a happy lather trying to relate the curious finds we made in the land to the Tudor cottage which stands (if that is the word for so relaxed and negligent a posture) upon it. Meanly, we have deprived them of this excitement by doing it ourselves.

The Floggit Bequest, though at first it seemed inexhaustible, was, in fact, quite soon worked out, so far as the major items went. The supply of nuts, bolts, screws and nails lasted for years. The scrap metal industry, and through it the export trade in a general way, has been enriched to the tune of a partial iron bedstead, a cistern, a mangle, one bicycle frame and pedal, several defective carburettors and magnetos of repellent primitiveness, a number of lorry wheelhubs and brake drums, segments of a flywheel, half of half a crankcase, a differential housing, and a Thing or two which I quite failed to identify. That was the work of our first digging season. But even after four or five years, we were still unearthing traces of an earlier civilization at the rate of one a week. Not a particularly genial civilization, it seems. A cut-glass decanter stopper raised our hopes momentarily, but the nearest we got to evidence of a gay old time was One Green Bottle. A handsome, even beautiful bottle: we thought the best of our predecessors until we found stamped on it the name of a mineral water maker. A set of fire irons speaks badly for the taste of an earlier generation. So does a china dog with the front paws missing. Incredibly, in these horsey surroundings, we have never found a single horse shoe. And now, I think, the soil is clear.

4

Spring

When the thaw came the birds went wild with joy. They are the first to feel the spring, and the most cruelly deluded when spring's earliest intimations play them false.

Some scientists say that it is not permissible to think of wild creatures in terms of human behaviour. But it is difficult not to do so. Birds behave most humanly. In easy times they display a highly developed social consciousness: critical, clannish, one might say almost snobbish. In hard times those cruel distinctions are forgotten, and they foregather at the kitchen door in mixed, humble groups, ready to forget, ready to accept not only the human presence but their own.

Only the indefatigably censorious robin resents this lowering of 'social standards'. He remains through the hardest weather truculent and resentful and possessive, and misses many a meal in his obsession with driving other birds from 'his' territory. He is also an unscrupulous opportunist, our robin. In the worst of the weather he flew indoors, plainly telling us that he could not be expected to share a meal with that scruffy mob of layabouts outside. An unhungry cat came waddling to see what was going on: cat and bird surveyed each other with wary but indulgent eyes, two opportunists face to face.

With the thaw came other intimations of spring. The savage weather is back for the moment, but we have seen enough to be reassured. The snowdrops that came out before the frost survive in flower, miraculously none the worse. Aconites are showing. Everywhere peeping up through the numbed sward are shoots promising spring; the unbelligerent but indomitable pale spears of daffodils, crocuses, bluebells and scillas.

The currant bushes are ruddy with fecund buds, and the long brown drooping fingers of willow trees, seen from an upstairs window, are speckled with new green. A weak sun behind the flowering currants shows their buds glowing like stained glass, a translucent ruby.

The daphne bushes by the kitchen door are in frail flower, the laburnum trees jolly with promises, and the stone-grey, lichen-loving wood of the forsythia is encrusted with buds about to break.

It is a pity to miss these shy signs that the year is on the turn. The casual human eye, almost fatally vulgarized by speed and stridency, can easily overlook them, seeing nothing but desolation in the waiting world. But the birds know. In these minute and modest signs, and in the new optimism of the birds' song, you can read the good news of the year. Though snow come late on highland and headland, we have seen with our own eyes the stealthy and subtle approach, ever nearer, and irrevocable, of spring.

Spring

It is like coming out of a tunnel. Suddenly you can *see*. You can see pale green blades of daffodils pushing up through black soil. You can see paeonies glowing with burning red spears of new life.

You can see the spring.

Winter is a sort of blindness or blinkers or a journey through a dark shaft. But once you have seen the spring you never let it out of your sight.

When we half-lived in a town flat without even a window-box we used to go again and again to the big cheap stores just to see the seed packets. Spring at sixpence a bag. Now with new eyes we see the new buds on spiraea and veronica and magnolia, and the apple trees are stirring. Double daisies open now, and the tough-yet-tender purple violas, that stayed in flower right up to the savage frost, are budding again already.

Now the spiked roller comes out to tame the shaggy lawn, and the oiled gleaming spade takes its first hungry bite of black loam. The first early peas and the broad beans are sown, and not even the voluptuous dividend of harvest-tide can match this moment.

Now the winter-wise house cat makes his first journeys afield, tasting the new air, knowing the signs. A farm cat like a tiger walks delicately along a hunter's hedgerow, and what those narrow yellow eyes are focused on is spring.

Birds, beasts and fishes know before we do. Salmon are in from the sea, forging upstream in swollen dark rivers to spawn in the same shallow stickles where their lives began. Sometimes when the wind drops the calm lake boils with the rings of rising trout. Maggot and chrysalis, mole and earthworm are astir.

Best of all, the day has won parity with the night. It is fifty-fifty now, and every day is longer than the last. The forces of darkness are in full retreat.

*   *   *   *

A Cottage Idyll

The steep flank of the ridge sheltered me from the sharp south-east wind, and by the time I breasted the summit I was warm again. The sun shone through bare trees and the wind rattled the branches.

When I found the track that winds along the ridge I turned with it towards the old shrine, and now the wind blew in my face. Leaning against it I remembered those who had taken this path before me.

This was the firm highway when all the land on either side was marsh, and along it pilgrims made their way to the shrine of their faith. If you have a feeling for history you cannot move in England without treading in the footsteps of your forbears, who made you what you are. To have no sense of the living past is to be isolated, imprisoned in your tiny world. It diminishes a man.

I was alone on the track but a great company went along with me. Then I came to a house standing by itself and in the potato plot alongside it a boat stood upside down. A man was working on this boat. I think he had worked a long time and was glad to rest, for he took a fill of tobacco and we talked of the sea lanes, while our pipe smoke shirred away merrily on the wind.

I asked him if he knew the turbulent seaways off Selsey Bill, and he knew them well. All his labour was directed to fitting out his boat so that when spring came riding in on the Atlantic wind he could sail that old tub close in under the crumbling ancient land of the Kingdom of Sussex. But when I asked him if he knew that Bishop Wilfred's palace lay under the sea off Selsey, he did not, nor had he heard of Wilfred, who taught the men of Sussex to make nets and in one stroke made Christians and fishermen of them all, as doubtless they are to this day.

He was mildly interested to know of these things and I could see that the next time he rode the seas off Sussex for his pleasure, that pleasure would be increased by his knowledge of what lay beneath his keel.

Spring

I left him working on his boat and after a long march with the wind rising I broke through a screen of beeches and saw below me a steading, first the church tower and then the farms and houses clustered around it, far below, and the rich land sloping very gently towards the river. There had been roofs down there for many centuries, the habitations of men who tilled the land and defended it when it was necessary to defend it. Beneath one of those ancient roofs there was a pot simmering and a fire burning, and to this I made my way, for I was tired now with the fresh cold wind and the walking.

Half in a waking dream of the past I came down the flank of the downs to the little house on its wise little knoll of dry land. I spoke of what I had seen and ate boiled beef and dumplings. Then I fell asleep, gazing into the caverns of the fire. But was vouchsafed no dreams.

* * * *

There are at least two aspects of gardening which reveal the gardener's character, or at any rate his temperament, as plainly as a session on a psychiatrist's couch. One is pruning. Pruning is a perfect give-away. Are you a slasher or a snipper? Your rose bushes tell all.

Nominally, at least, our roses are my concern. True, I have to be reminded to get out there with the spray-gun, later in the year. I am by nature a non-belligerent gardener, content to live and let live, and perhaps unduly tolerant of the innumerable pests which keep chemists rich and busy. But I never need to be urged to get going with the secateurs. The sergeant-major instinct, often dormant in the most demure, comes right out at pruning time. Some kindly, undogmatic people don't possess it at all. Naturally reluctant to bash and bully, they tentatively trim off the tips and put their trust in the rose bush's inherent decency and gratitude. Which is naive though nice.

Not so the bashers and slashers, the This Is For Your Own

A Cottage Idyll

Good gang, the It Hurts Me More Than It Hurts You party (to which, I find with a touch of surprise and disgust, I belong). When we have finished pruning, all that remains of a rosebush is two or three forlorn stunted sticks. I would not claim that our roses are better for it, but *we* are.

Grass is the other give-away. There is no argument about the proper texture of a lawn – the more remorselessly you cut and roll it the better it is. But what about the edges? Some like straight, parade-tidy edges, cut off sharp and square like paving stones. Others, while approving the square-cut edge, prefer meandering curves. In this one matter you can see a grave difference of temperaments. But there is a still deeper difference. There are those who detest both the straight line and the square-cut edge, and prefer the grass to merge, as imperceptibly as surf, into some other form of natural growth. These are the people, tender and affectionate characters all, who edge their grass with pinks, aubretia, alyssum, arabis. To the chagrin of the luckless mortal who has to keep it tidy.

Though confessedly a brutal pruner, I must say I am all for the informal, the meandering, the curving edge and the ill-defined frontier between grass and other growths. There is altogether too much regimentation in the world for my liking, and it increases all the time. In the garden, at any rate, we can let life's irrepressible preference for curves get the better of man's puritanical passion for straight lines.

*   *   *   *

The sun shines, but in April the water is still cold. In these up-country rivers, flowing down from peaty moors, thin water purling fast over gravel and stones, the trout are ready before you are.

Socks, thick stockings, rubber-proofed waders . . . still you feel the upland cold squeezing your shins. As you wade in deeper, slow and cunning, sliding on the stones, you feel it grip your thighs.

Spring

But with the minty water smells in your nostrils and the sun on your face you get out line and begin your casts. You don't need to learn to cast, you need to unlearn. Just a rolling switch of the supple rod as the line comes down, so fast in the racing water. Just a rod's length of line ahead of you, and beyond that the spider-web cast with its team of flies, searching the lies behind the stones.

What flies? It depends where you are, who you are, what you believe. Whatever it is, you believe it more devoutly than the catechism. Maybe you pin your faith on a team of sparsely hackled spiders, black or smoky blue. Or the classic silver-bodied March Brown on the point, with the gold-ribbed Hare's Ear on the dropper and the cheeky Coch-y-Bhonddu on the bob. Maybe the Snipe and Purple, or the Waterhen Bloa. It matters little if you believe. It is the team you follow.

Too soon yet. No response. An hour drifts by in a dream. Time now to shove the rod butt down your waders and roll a cigarette, or fill a pipe. Smoke was never so blue, never smelled so sweet. Time to look at the burgeoning thorns, the sally bushes and willows that are the fisherman's friends. A jay flashes across the green-brown bank and into the hanging wood. Halcyon the kingfisher dazzles you. Harry the heron rises ahead, a bag of bones dressed in rags, hating you; a rival disturbed, flapping away to a farther beat.

The day warms up and still your feet are cool in the weltering water. The touch comes. You know it was a touch, and your slack hand missed it. (The winter behind you.) Tensed now, all attention, you try it again, and this time the cunning left hand sweeps away from the butt, the line snakes back through the rings and the rod tip springs into its tensely quivering arc. This is the moment. You have him on. The day's first, and the year's.

In the explosive moment of wild fear and exhilaration you know all over again the catalogue and testament of angling's tragic and irresistible joys.

A Cottage Idyll

He is soon beaten. You hold him in your hand, the spotted one, so bright and firm. You ease out the priest, the stick of ash rolled in lead, and with one blow kill him, trying not to look him in the eye, the eye that goes veiled and smoky as one quiver shakes him and he lies still.

'Butcher, butcher!' cries the kingfisher. 'Butcher, butcher!' cry the heron and the jay. They are butchers too, and think you have robbed them. They are marauders, and you have out-marauded them. Kinder than the abattoir, quicker and more merciful by far than the trawlerman with his flapping mounds emptied on to icy decks. Yet this moment sticks in your throat. Sticks in your throat, convulses your glottis. Your heart is beating faster, another heart is still.

You take out your knife and rip the belly from vent to gills. The inwards come out in a coherent sprawl, you toss them behind you in the gliding water. Eels will have them before they travel far.

You put the trout in the wicker creel and wash your hands in the water. When you straighten up you look at the pearly sky, stippled with clouds. For a moment you are giddy. You get out line again and start to fish. Eyes are watching you from everywhere, the vole peers from his hole in the bank, wren and kingfisher and jay know all about you, the biggest predator. The innumerable voices of the waterside, that paused for a moment – or did you imagine that? – brawl on again.

You force yourself to think prudentially, commonsensically, of supper: firm carcases slashed and grilled, with butter, and lemon, and brown bread-and-butter. You have a function here. The ecology of the river valley, infinitely complex, built up in interlocking layer upon layer of necessary organic life, predators and preyed-upon . . . its beauty, its wild exhilaration, is an accident of your species. You happen to be a man.

The line is snaking out again, the rolling line whispers as it goes by your ear. There is a corpse in your creel and in the living water living creatures lurk behind the stones, killing what they can. Can you bear to kill? Can you bear to live? You fish on, the fluent rhythm healing your soul's scars, sprung with excitement and acceptance. This is the mystery, this is the benediction.

*   *   *   *

There are two theories about the unknown genius who designed our coal store. One is that he was an emaciated dwarf who walked on all fours and had a remarkable talent for seeing in the dark. The other is that he just didn't believe in coal fires.

If I told you the dimensions you wouldn't believe them. It is absurdly long and at no point is it wider than the door. Nobody carrying a scuttle can turn round in it. As that ripe character Bill Maynard used to say, when you're in, you're in. To fill a hod of coal you climb up two steps, open the door, and take out a bucket, two trowels, a border fork, a hoe, a hank of raffia, a bundle of garden canes, and a pair of gumboots. These you place outside. You then start your long trudge towards the small heap of coal, barely visible in the distance. The wind blows the door shut and you might just as well be down a mine.

You back down again, stumbling on bits of anthracite and brushing your clean shirt-sleeves against the walls. You open the door with your behind: inelegant, but, since you can't turn round, the only way.

Going forward again, you fall over the scuttle.

When you've filled it, you start the backing-out game again, feeling like Victor Silvester going slow, slow, quick; the quick being when you go down the steps before you realize you've reached them.

The coalmen are very fond of our coalhouse, very fond indeed. When we hear their lorry in the lane everybody is mobilized for a rush job. If we are lucky, we get the bucket, the trowels, the border fork, the hoe, the raffia, the canes and the gumboots out in the nick of time. Kay strings an auxiliary clothes-line from kitchen to coalhouse. The first time the coalman came, a tall, bowed figure with a sack on his back, the clothes-line took the sack off as neat as ninepence. So the line has to come down. Even so, there can be trouble. The other day he got wedged in the doorway, or at least his sack did. An embarrassing situation.

We have a second store, for coke, at the bottom of the garden. It used to serve another and more elemental purpose. One of my first jobs when we moved here was to convert it, which I did with a clothes peg on my nose.

The old door was pretty rotten. I had a brain-wave and sawed it horizontally into two halves, like a stable door. I won't claim that it has been a complete success. If the level within is high, then when you open the top half, coke cascades out over the aubretia. If the level is low, you have to fold yourself like a jacknife and bend right down with the upper edge of the bottom half sticking in your stomach and the blood pounding in your ears and spiders falling into your hair, while you scrape about with a shovel.

We daren't open the bottom half; we should never get it shut. In fact it's boarded up, though any day now the whole thing will burst open.

Well, let it.

*   *   *   *

The man and the dog and the pigeon live in a cottage with pointed Gothic windows, like a chapel, and a green door. It stands on a sharp slope nicely out of flood's reach, above shallow murmuring rapids marked on old maps as *Ford*, though in fact a three-plank footbridge spans them now. I have seen some desirable residences but few more desirable than this, even though it is oil-lit and every day the man has to go down to the river with buckets for his water. There are many dafter ways of spending time, and anyway his dog goes with him. His dog goes with him everywhere and their friend the pigeon watches them.

We had worked our way upstream picking up a fish here and there though it was still cold and there was no hatch of the lovely gossamer water-flies which fight their indomitable way up out of the mud into the light of day to live briefly, splendidly, passionately. But when you haven't seen the trout stream for six months the first sight of it in April is so beautiful and thrilling that it almost hurts. In fact it does hurt, in the way of lovely and poignant experiences in which memory is mixed up with anticipation. It is a very bearable pain.

We sat down by the rapids to rest and eat and there were a pair of yellow wagtails bobbing and bowing on the stones. They didn't mind us. They were absorbed in each other.

The pigeon was damn near as big as a seagull. It was sitting on the roof ridge all alone, watching, and it rose and circled to greet the man and the dog when they came out of the wood that runs down to the river on the far bank.

The man and the dog crossed the stream and went into the cottage and they came out again with a lot of bread. They put some on the bird table in the steeply-sloping garden, which was beautifully tilled, and the pigeon flopped down to eat of it.

The man sat down on the ground: he just sat down plonk as if the ground were a luxurious armchair. The dog jumped up on to the man's shoulders.

For quite a time they all sat there chewing away, then the pigeon flapped back on to the roof.

The man wore old grey flannels and a green jersey and a peaked cap tipped forward over his eyes, which had many wrinkles round them from long looking. He had a long jaw and he was as brown as a piece of walnut. The dog was a mongrel with a plump white body and a brown patch over one eye, and a keen pretty little face.

A Cottage Idyll

They had been hunting together in the wood and now they were resting after food, watching the water.

This is the way they were, the last I saw of them. The man was sitting cross-legged on the steep slope with his elbows on his knees and his chin in his hands. The dog sat on his shoulders looking over his head. The pigeon sat on the roof.

Those three sat looking down at the running water, watching the water purling past their home. Blue smoke rose from the chimney as the sun went down. We left and then they were all alone.

*   *   *   *

The sun broke through and everybody who could went out to work under a high pearly sky, and the south wind blew softly and suddenly everybody remembered spring. That is to say everybody who was old enough. To my certain knowledge there were two young cats who had never seen a spring, and a whole new generation of birds.

But of course there is such a thing as ancestral memory and all these young things were possessed by the ancestral memory of spring and went slightly mad with joy that wells up within and cannot be explained nor counterfeited. This is the possessing and transfiguring joy which fills you suddenly without any cause that you can put down in words. It is rare and wonderful and I'm afraid it is soon forgotten.

It has possessed me when I have been walking in a city street without a penny in my pocket. I felt it once during an examination, sitting in a vast dim hall writing inaccurate and unimportant answers. It may take you at any time and it is like a benediction. This is the simple joy of being alive and it makes all that you do pleasurable and all that you own unimportant.

To hear the spade going into the dark earth was as good as music, wild and exhilarating. The flames fiercely consumed dross and rubbish and the fertilizing ash will go back into the earth. We all got dirty, which is the way to enjoy cleanliness. We got tired, which is the way to enjoy rest. We got hungry, which is the way to enjoy food.

When the light failed we took a lingering look at the newly gleaming earth and the snowdrops and aconites and the bulbs thrusting up under the willow, and those of us who live in trees and hedgerows went back to their trees and hedgerows, and those of us who live in houses went back indoors.

At night a friend came to sit with us by the fire of logs and he too had felt the transfiguring touch that day as he stood atop bare cliffs looking south towards the source of spring. He told us how the sea-birds behaved joyfully over the margin of land and water, riding the mild swinging stream of air as buoyant as boats. They, too, were possessed by the promise, like the singers who had gathered in tremulous choirs on the warm south slope of the cottage roof. It was wonderful, he said, to stand on the uttermost limit of the land and feel on your face the warming wind from Africa. For no man is isolated in his own patch who feels on his skin the momentous travelling wind.

We spoke prudently of hard weather to come, just to prove that we were experienced and sceptical and not to be taken in by one fine day. But it was just a bit of ritual, propitiating Fate. We make these gestures of distrust to protect our ordinary selves from disappointment and the cynic's mockery. But, in fact, none of those living creatures who shared the sun that day would ever be quite the same again. For though there is hard weather ahead, spring never goes back on its word.

*   *   *   *

If the fat bumble bee will leave me in peace for a while I can settle down here under the willow tree and get on with earning my living. That bee has taken it upon himself, for no reason at all, to lord it over the garden. There is always some officious busybody among our unpaying guests who fancies himself as Lord of the Manor.

Last year it was an aldermanic robin who elected himself First Citizen. But although he was a lad who could not be left out of anything – always perching on garden tools and chairs and toddling around two paces in the rear – at least he reserved his bad temper for other birds. He rather gave the impression of sucking up to us.

Now this bee is a different type again. He has got it in for us, I can't imagine why. You can hardly go for an innocent stroll without being buzzed, dive-bombed, and in various bee ways molested.

In flight he seems about as big as a wren, so you will readily imagine that being buzzed by this particular bee is a shade unnerving. I have no idea where he lives – he has appeared out of thin air to give me a buzz in every corner of the plot – but I know where he wants to live. He wants to live in the kitchen. Several times Kay has slammed the door in his face in the nick of time. One day soon he is bound to make it and then he will have to be turned out, for no cottage is big enough to hold us all. Compared with which operation, the time we caught the bat in my landing net will seem in retrospect like a gentle game.

It is too much to hope that this vast and irritable bee will find a soul-mate and settle down. The love life of bees is a sad story altogether. By contrast the loving of birds seems to me wholly delightful and their domestic arrangements admirable.

The garden belongs to the birds just now. Later they will be less in evidence and the incomparable joy of their love-song will have diminished to the everyday conversation of humdrum domesticity. But now, while trees and hedgerows are putting on their new immaculate green, in the days of the daffodils and tulips and the cherry blossom and violets, now the garden is to the birds.

Spring

Tremulous and ecstatic they haunt the crystal air of spring, flashing across the little enclave of our plot in swooping flight that expresses in every curve and line the very essence of the awakening creative hour. Oblivious, uncalculating, fond and free; each in his living a reproach and perhaps an inspiration to the self-destructive, haggard, life-destroying world of men. Each in his living both artist and lover.

*   *   *   *

I shall have to have my logging saw sharpened again. It has had a lot of use lately. Luckily I have a friend who sets a saw a fair treat. It isn't everybody who can. I have never been too good at sharpening edge tools myself, though I can take an edge off as fast as most.

I bought this old saw while we were still living in the brick jungle, just after the war, with never a log to saw and nowhere to saw it if we had had. I bought it strictly for the name – a perfect example of the power of propaganda. 'The Lumberjack Saw', it was called. It is one of those rugged affairs with a blade joining the two ends of a frame made of bent steel tubing. I can still see the coloured placard in the ironmonger's shop, with a highly romanticized picture of two strapping young men in check shirts tearing their way through a primeval forest. In the background, as I recall it, one of their mates was frying enormous steaks over a wood fire. . . .

Naturally this appealed to every thwarted instinct. I put down my money and carried the lumberjack saw home, where it was the occasion of some pretty pithy wit. (Don't try saying that aloud.)

For some years the lumberjack saw hung in various London flats, looking highly incongruous and freely regarded as a monument to my gullibility and lack of thrift. It was almost worse than useless. We owned no other saw, and occasionally we needed one, as all households do, from time to time. Then the lumberjack model, with teeth nearly half an inch long – well, say a quarter – was pressed into service on jobs that really wanted a fretsaw.

But its day came. Through the years of waiting it stood as a symbol, if you like, of the sort of atmosphere I really wanted to breathe. We had hardly moved to the country cottage before I was out with it, ripping down trees and converting them into logs, and wasn't it hard work!

Of course, there is a snag to the use of the lumberjack. It is really, strictly speaking, a two-handed saw. When it comes to choosing a partner for the other end of a two-handed saw you are up against it. Lifelong friendship is no guarantee of success. Your mate must not only try just about as hard as you try. He or she must also be just about your match in height, reach and energy. Any conspicuous disparity leads rapidly to accusations of bad faith. It is as delicate a situation as holding the mouth of a sack while somebody shovels stuff in.

Nowadays I use the lumberjack single-handed. And no longer do I feel anything like those colourful young men in the picture. Nothing makes you feel your age faster than sawing logs. Still, it does give you an appetite for that steak.

*　　*　　*　　*

In the time of the year when lilac is in bloom, and old-fashioned wallflowers, and bluebells and lilies of the valley, you can stand with your back to the trunk of the willow tree and wait for the swallows. You part the hanging fronds that touch the grass, and enter a natural tent, or wigwam. It is cool in here. Leaning against the trunk you can see what goes on in the great inverted bowl of sky, but you cannot very easily be seen, especially in your nondescript greeny-brown clothing of shirt and slacks. When you enter into the world of the willow you acquire a certain privacy and a certain peace.

And here you await the swallows.

Spring

Noble and gallant birds, so beautiful and so brave: to see them arrive is one of the great events of our year. It is very fine to be human and civilized, but when you consider the swallows' prodigious flight, their courage and faithfulness and grace, you are not quite so prone to ascribe all the virtues exclusively to the human kind.

But the longer you live away from the racket of towns, the more you realize that many of what we are pleased to call specifically human virtues are present in the animal world, at least in rudimentary form. And also some of the vices. We are not entirely a race apart, but are linked in kinship with everything that lives. Of course, it does not follow that we must like all our relations!

Another event of the year, between the cuckoo and the swallow, is the song of the skylark. Even lovelier, perhaps, than the song of nightingales in the dense primrose woods that stretch from the edge of the village towards the little river, the song and the singer rise together, joyous and aspiring, until they vanish in the blue sky. There comes a moment when you can still hear the song, followed by a moment when it is gone. There is a moment when you can still see the bird, a black dot in heaven, and a moment when you can see it no longer. But you can never be absolutely precise about that moment. It is not clear-cut.

So it is with all memories and all partings.

So it will be when the swallows fly south. So it is when you say goodbye to a friend.

The grass grows imperceptibly over the abandoned road, and just as surely forgetfulness steals in. There comes a moment when you cannot really recall the face.

What is left, then? Ah, perhaps *that* is where we differ from animal kind. Out of physical oblivion you recall qualities of mind and heart; acts of affection, a way of thinking. And maybe you are changed by what you remember.

Birds aspire only to be birds, humans want to be more

than human. And in the process of wanting, sometimes become less.

*   *   *   *

Riding in a horsebox is glamorous and fine. People slow down and give you right of way, and look up at you with interest and respect. You might only have an old sow in the back, but then again you might have a real live race-horse; and motorists are naturally more considerate to racehorses than to people.

We did have a real racehorse in Farmer White's box, as it happens, and we were taking him to a point-to-point meeting. I found the situation slightly unreal, since the nearest I ever got to an understanding with a horse was on a sultry evening in Llantwit Major many years ago, when I offered a horse a saccharine tablet and he bit me.

The bookies had set up their cheerful garish stands in a row, and sumptuous cars owned by credulous yobbos, and of course others, were lined up along the finishing straight. The park was looking its best, impeccably fresh and green, and the river which I know to be full of trout flowed in a great arc round the course, and the grey mansion on its eminence brooded over all.

I was supposed to locate Kay, who was with Farmer White's party somewhere down the course, but frankly I spent more time than was considered seemly in listening to snatches of conversation which puzzled me, in my ignorance. 'They'll be on top of the ground today' was my favourite, but 'He's got a leg at each corner' was pretty intriguing, too.

I might have made a little packet had I been content to follow the advice of my companion. Alan put me on the winner of every race but one. I backed them all, in modest two-bobs at the Tote, but since I could not resist backing several other horses in each race, too, purely on the strength of their names or the looks of the lady riders, my total profit was not quite so substantial as it might have been. Say five bob.

Even so, I did better than Kay, who backed according to the colour of the jockeys' outfits, and squandered a disagreeably large proportion of the housekeeping money on such fetching rigs as Blue, Old Gold Sleeves and Sash, Black Cap. This aesthetic betting is a snare and a delusion.

There were hitches, of course; our day would hardly be complete without them. There was a nasty moment when I joined a group standing at the tailboard of a station wagon laden with food and drink. I was under the impression the stuff was for sale, and waited my turn with exemplary patience until a certain coolness in the atmosphere tipped me off that this was a particularly well-equipped private party.

It was a lovely day; it showed us an aspect of English country life which we had not seen before. All was serene, mildly gay, fresh and rather beautiful. It was possible to forget everything unpleasant; and, wisely, we did.

No one mentioned – what was the point? – that the great grey mansion in the park was now a reformatory school for boys. No one paid any attention if distant grey figures appeared for a moment on the far side of the river, beyond the pale.

*   *   *   *

It never comes on to blow fresh out of the North-west on an April day but I see again in the mind's eye, flashing past, all the turbulent and beautiful waterways that I have known. All the bays and headlands, all the races of the narrow sea, all the estuaries and havens, and the streams that feed them.

So when the sky blackened and the wind rose, though shafts of sunlight from behind a cloud illuminated the flowering cherry and the daffodils and the mown grass and the greening trees, so then for a moment I saw none of those comely sights, but a more distant vision. Or, rather, I saw the two together, as if fused and held in a startling revelation of double-sight; the near and the far, the now and the then, the secure and homely together with the remote and hazardous. And this is something that happens ever oftener as life goes on. But particularly on a chequered April day when the willow fronds stream out wildly and beautifully in the keen wind, and clouds pour like cataracts down the dizzy slopes of the sky. No doubt it is a very fine thing to have come to the haven, with a snug old place to sleep in and a ha'porth of land around it to give you room to breathe your own air. This is a grand snug life now and I like it well. But I should not like it one half so much, no, not one hundredth, if there were not another sort of experience behind it to give it the enormous zest of comparison.

And you feel this most keenly on an April day because April itself is the great month of contrast.

The light is not the same for ten minutes together, the wind is as variable as the light, the temperature is up and down, and you are near enough to winter to remember vividly the numbing winter deadness of land and light.

No wonder April is the month of memories. Man is a land animal but long ago he came out of the sea, or so they say, and there are plenty like me who come fully alive only within earshot of running water. This must be the stirring of an ancestral memory, as deep as an eel's. It is a strange attraction, composed in equal parts of love and fear. Wading along a slippery ledge of rock where the maddened river foams and pours through a constricting gorge, I am at least as much frightened as exhilarated, and long to be safe ashore. But being ashore is nothing without the wading-in. It is the same in a little boat. Undoubtedly the best moments are pushing off from the haven and tying up again. What lies between those two high points may be wonderful, or it may be terrible. And it may be both. Only one thing is sure. You can't enjoy the one without the other.

April is the time of year when you remember all the times

you prayed to be safe and dry and still. You savour your present safety and snugness and stillness all the more because you recall the other times.

*   *   *   *

Any time now, I shall go down to the sea to visit an old man who lives in a boat. I don't know that I would call him a seafaring man. He may have been; but he does not talk about his past. Now he lives in this small, old boat that never puts to sea. It lies up a creek and the tide greets it twice a day. At low tide it is all aground. At high water the stern floats, but the bows are tied to a tree and grass grows round the prow.

Once, standing by his boat and looking seawards down the creek, I saw five herons fishing, standing silent and still in the shallow water. The old man and the herons live as best they may, on the margins of the sea. There are no fat herons. It is a fine way to live if you have the heart for it.

I would buy bait from the old man if he would dig it. But he is lazy, even lazier than I am. He enjoys watching while I dig painfully in stiff black clay laced with flints as sharp as knives. I would rather he had the money and he would rather I had the work. To that extent, we understand each other. I hope that when I am old I shall have the strength of mind to live as idly.

The trouble with most people is that they always want something to happen. They are intoxicated by events. The old man has no interest in events. Not what you might call events. The tide makes and ebbs, the downs are sometimes sharp-clear and sometimes veiled. Bass and eels run up the estuary and flounders inhabit it. It rains or is dry. Wildfowl fly over.

To be aware of these things is an eventful life in itself.

Do not picture in your mind a dainty little craft with polished brasswork and chintzy curtains. The old man does not care for appearances. He has 'let himself go', as the saying is. He looks

103

a rough old customer and you might say he lives in squalor. It depends on your definition. Some would say that the view from his porthole is worth £1,000 a year. It is a matter of taste.

Well, there it is. He lives there, in a sort of boat, and I doubt if he cares very much what anybody thinks. Weathered, taciturn, and sardonic, the old man lives his own life on the outer fringe of the human world. I don't suppose it would make any difference to him, one way or another, if I failed to turn up this spring. But it would make a difference to me if he were gone.

Once in a while I enjoy the salutary and terrifying experience of looking at a free man.

*   *   *   *

Alf Norman the forester has a fine fire going in the clearing by his hut. On this wind, a cool one from the North Sea, woodsmoke drifts across to us in fitful aromatic gusts. In between the pungent gusts of woodsmoke you can smell the delicate keen scent of new-mown grass.

This reminds me that we are always going to build a lean-to and spreader of oak stakes, so that we can smoke the fish we catch over a surly slow smouldering of oak shavings. But that is one of those things which may never get done. We catch so few fish nowadays. The hunting spirit is almost completely exorcised. Do not ask what takes its place. It may return. Meanwhile we eat fish caught by other men heaving on the hostile ocean; and with every mouthful you can taste the flavour of their strenuous lives.

All the blossom at once drove down in the north-east wind. Apple blossom lay on the grass like large confetti, each disc dry and brittle and beginning to turn brown. It piled up in every crevice of the warm-coloured, sagging old roof, and lay in little wind-tapered drifts at the foot of every tree.

The very old gnarled apple trees gave up their multitudinous magnificence of blossom, the new young trees lost their first few tender flakes of flower, the cherry and the damsons were all stripped bare in the same long set of wind.

Now Kay is sweeping up blossom in the concrete gully between the garage and the low wall of stones and flints that keeps the orchard bank from crumbling and sliding down. A cotoneaster pinned to the garage wall contributes its quota of minute blossom, as small as seeds. They take some sweeping! Once you start trying to impose the human notion of order and tidiness on the natural world, you have a job for life. Nature is magnificently untidy. I take comfort from this thought.

A letter from a friend who hates writing, that is an event to be thankful for. It says that the spiny silver bass are inshore again, hunting the young salmon and sea-trout smolts descending from their parent river to make the great compulsive adventure in the ocean. Shall we row out again together over the sandy bar where the tide breaks in a line of creaming foam, out to the wrecking reefs where tides rip and roar? I should like to think so. Water calls mysteriously. There is no denying its call. It pulls like a magnet. Yet I do not particularly want to hunt the hunters. Strange how you come to make peace.

The forester's fire is burning low. Acorn to sapling, sapling a tree, tree to ash. Now the ash will nourish the soil again. Nothing is lost. Birth and death, gain and loss are incidents without cosmic meaning. It is a commonwealth.

$$* \qquad * \qquad * \qquad *$$

As soon as I began to dig a robin appeared from nowhere to keep me company.

He was a rather ragged robin, fluffy and pale – the youngest, I dare say, of all the innumerable generations of his family which have lived their lives in 'our' little plot. They have the best title to this space: it was their home before it was mine or any man's.

I dug a narrow strip of soil for the spinach beet and the robin

A Cottage Idyll

followed me down the row, parallel with the tall fence of sweet peas and the growing hedge of beech and hornbeam. Working our way down this narrow strip the robin and I were quite cut off from the world.

'Had I but world enough and time . . .' the poet sang. We had all the world we wanted and all the time. Absorbed in our work, picking at the friable, crumbling treasure of black soil, we made the small companionable clicking noises of fork and beak, and there were no other sounds at all except the swishing sound of the wind.

At last it was all shipshape, the wonderful fine tilth inviting the seeds. The seeds of spinach beet are fascinating in themselves; withered, whiskery-looking, shrunken little globes with a hundred flat and curving facets; a geometer's delight. In they went, and the soil closed over them: the elementary act of faith, the first holy rite, the bit of gardening which I like best.

I warned the robin, in language far from mild, what would happen to him if he disturbed the seeds. He showed no sign of taking my blood-curdling threats seriously, and watched curiously while I gathered twigs and wove a deterrent network of black cotton over the seed row. This is the bit of gardening which I like least. But there's no help for it.

As I straightened my back the lane filled with a vast hubbub and confusion. Big cars, small cars, a coach and several vans were pulled up, in a long convoy, and out of them poured a race of men as odd-looking, in our old lane, as visitors from Space. Young men with wispy beards and crewcuts and strange hair styles, wearing jeans, sweaters, casual suede shoes. Young men carrying weird pieces of equipment and crying shrilly in a weird jargon. Young men, in short, who make films.

For a space of time the fragrant air was full of the nervous twittering talk of film-making men. The tractor and the milk lorry edged their way past the traffic jam. Rumour flashed about the village. Hair was hastily combed.

Spring

Then, as suddenly as they had appeared, the film men vanished. Heaven knows what prodigious feat of organization lay behind their coming and going. One moment they filled the lane. The next, they were gone.

Wondering if I had dreamed it all, I went back to the newly dug row behind the sweet peas. The young robin was perched on the pea sticks. He flew down to my feet and greeted me with his little chirrup. We were on our own again.

*   *   *   *

Do you believe in spirits? No, not ghosts: they are real enough, heaven knows. I mean the spirits that inform places and the spirits that drive men to their destiny. The spirit of place is the same, I think, for all men. The other day on the blue height of the hills that wall off Wales I renewed my acquaintance with a spirit of place that did more than any other to shape me. There is no part of Britain that feels quite like the March of Wales. You do not have to know the history of the March to understand this spirit, but when you know the story, it confirms what you feel in your bones. Frontiers all feel the same, especially when they have been much fought over, as most of them have.

But the spirit of place is a chained thing: you are out of its reach once you turn that significant corner that comes in every road. Whereas the spirits that drive men to their destiny are alive and kicking. They kick you up the ladder or down the slippery slope. There is the spirit of fire, that produces pyromaniacs and stokers and cooks and blacksmiths and maybe firemen. The spirit of air, that makes fliers and pigeon fanciers, bird watchers and a particular sort of poet. The earth spirit, driving the peasant and the lady with secateurs and the man who trudges home from an allotment through twilit streets, not seeing the smoke-stained bricks. I believe there is a special spirit of trees, and a strong spirit of the wind that makes rebels, and perhaps a spirit of speed sent to make men mad. And there must be a malignant spirit that makes misers. These things I guess at from what I see.

But of one powerful spirit I can speak with certainty, though with awe; for it rules me. It is the very ancient water spirit, that makes sailors and fishermen, swimmers and beachcombers and bridge-builders and pirates. And possibly plumbers. When a drought breaks there are none happier than those whom the water spirit rules, for the brotherliness of rain is felt unmistakably by one who hates and fears parched earth and dust and deserts.

A green gorgeousness stretched all the wet way from Wales. The many-coloured pasture gleamed like paint. Back home the new grass which we had sown was springing, each blade still separate and proud. The little world we live in smelled of water, there was water underfoot in the squelch and spring of turf and there was the softness of water in the breathed air. This is the perfection of weather for one who is governed by the water spirit. Gurgling gutters and glistening hedgerows are all of one piece with waterfall and weir, pond and estuary, the long loneliness of lakes, and the excitement, which is truly enchantment, of steep swift rivers racing to the sea.

Of course, such talk of governing spirits is unfashionable and unpopular, if not absurd. In this blithe Age of Reason people believe in psychology and statistics. But not in spirits. Not even in the spirits that inhabit joy. I am centuries out of date. My luck holds.

* * * *

News from the sea told that bass were close inshore and the wind was off the land. But my sea crew who defy sea-sickness and salt spray and the noonday dazzle of sun on heaving water, my hardy and jolly sea crew were laid low. The young 'un lay in a big hospital ward being fed through tubes, and the old 'un lay in a small hospital ward being dosed with drugs. My sea crew laid low and the holiday beginning and bass sighted in the

estuary, avid and piratical. Sitting by sick beds talking of the
sea and fishes with my friends, until peremptory bells rang and
visitors were ushered out. . . . A sad start to a summer holiday.

We were none too pleased. We had abandoned a long adventurous journey, planned for years, because petrol was rationed
and the future unpredictable. The moment our holiday was
over petrol was freed. However, there was a gleam of wicked
consolation when we listened to the news one tingling morning,
sitting in the white kitchen that needed a coat of paint, and
the chap said that the exact spot where we should have been
fishing for salmon had had the distinction that night of eleven
degrees of frost.

Well, there remained the kitchen that needed a lick of paint.
But after a few years you get sick of slapping white paint on top
of white paint. Just who thought of the change first is still a
matter for discussion, but never mind, we both agreed that this
was the moment to break away from the perfectionist tyranny of
clinical white. Perhaps we had seen too many hospitals.

We drove into the town as if we were going on holiday and
we bought saxe-blue paint and bright red paint and ivory paint
and new brushes and turpentine. We drove home singing and we
brewed strong coffee and set to work craftily with very small
brushes. Perhaps it doesn't sound much of a holiday; but there
it is, we enjoyed it to the full. I'm not what you'd call house-
proud. I could live in a log cabin and like it, if it happened to
be in the right place and with the right company. All the same,
every room has a potential personality of its own, and it is fun
to draw it out, encourage it, flatter it. Rather like making the
most of a woman by praising her good points and encouraging
her to experiment. The right man can make even a plain woman
beautiful.

Well, the plain old kitchen suddenly lit up and began to look
like a place to live in, and that is all right because we do live in it
a good deal, though it is pretty damned inconvenient really.

A Cottage Idyll

But it's remarkable how even inanimate things respond to a little affection. The old place is good to us and we've done it a favour in return, and I don't call it a wasted holiday at all, though there's my sea crew laid low and the boat high and dry in the creek.

*   *   *   *

A stranger appeared in the village and began to nail road signs to the walls, without a word. He worked with the speed and stealth of a man laying a charge of high-explosive. Then he vanished, as mysteriously as he had appeared. But the village will never be quite the same again. Now, for the first time since civilization came to Surrey, we are more or less on the map.

When you come ambling up the green lane from Ripley which ends in a T-junction at what we are pleased to call 'The Street' you are confronted by a vivid great sign nailed on the wall of Mrs Illing's cottage. LEATHERHEAD, it says, leering to the left. GUILDFORD, grimacing to the right.

At first sight this was disturbing to ostriches like me, for one of the charms of our village was its complete lack of obvious contact with the outer world. Now one is daily reminded that *some*body, *some*where, knows about us. However, it could be worse. You will notice that the signs only direct travellers *out* of the village. It is still pretty difficult to get *into* it, as innumerable would-be visitors will testify.

Our village was preserved from progress by the happy accident of lying between two main roads. If you want to reach it from the Portsmouth road you need a compass and a favourable wind and the luck of Riley. If you want to get into it from the Leatherhead–Guildford road, you have the choice of two signs. One says TO THE QUEEN'S HEAD. The other says TO SURREY ISOLATION HOSPITAL. I would not want to influence the traveller in his choice.

It speaks well for the dogged adventurousness of the race that strangers do, in fact, quite frequently turn up in the village. Whether they make it by dead reckoning, astro-navigation, or blind chance, I do not know. But every weekend we see numbers of lost souls sauntering through, looking left and right for a tea shop and finding nothing more nourishing than a strong smell of silage.

Not to put too fine a point on it, our village is somewhat less effusively welcoming than a holiday camp. At one and the same time it illustrates why townspeople save up all their lives to retire to the country *and* why there is a drift from the land. As far as looks go, we have almost everything; a super-abundance of natural beauty and some pleasant architecture. But you can't live on looks. The 'amenities' tot up to one fine but rather empty church, one less fine but less empty inn, one school, one hall and one shop.

We still hug the illusion that we are a self-contained and self-sufficing community, and many of us would not willingly live elsewhere. But the new signposts point the way. The plain truth is that the life of the village depends absolutely on the infernal combustion engine, the storage battery, and the power station. In the television age, isolation is illusion.

*   *   *   *

You can take it on the authority of my wife, no less, that when she heard the sound of heavy footsteps and heavy breathing at the side of the house, she assumed that prayer had been answered and the dustmen had actually arrived.

She was still washing-up, reflecting (I daresay) on the excellence of the British way of life in general and the Rural District Council in particular, when there stepped neatly on to the lawn, before her eyes, a bull.

Now I must, in fairness to the ladies who took part in the ensuing little drama, and in view of certain suggestions made to me of which you will hear more later, affirm that never for a moment did Kay or her friend Lily doubt the identity of this beast. To them it was a bull, indisputably and horribly a bull, from the first instant.

It says much for the tranquillizing effect of life with Wiggin that Kay did not drop a dish. It seems that it did not even occur to her to dial 999, nor to call up the farmer and demand, in a sharp voice, that he remove his property from ours. (A course which the master of the house would certainly have taken, prudently locked in his study.)

Instead, Kay put down the teapot and went out to reason with the bull.

It was at this moment that Lily appeared, through the gap in the sketchy fence which separates her garden from ours, to find her way barred by the bull. She promptly observed – I would not believe this had not Kay told me herself – 'Go along, there, you horrible thing! Shoo!'

It is probable that the bull was taken aback by this mode of address. At any rate, he shambled meekly towards the house. Kay then deflected him from his obvious intention to enter the kitchen by waving a trowel and uttering the memorable formula. 'Here, where d'you think you're going? My goodness!'

The bull must have realized that he was up against two remarkable women. He strolled quietly towards the lane, taking the northerly side of this house. Kay took the southerly side, and beat him to the front gate by what she afterwards referred to, without irony, as a short head.

There then occurred a procession towards the heart of the village which I would have given something to see. Kay led the way, uttering ladylike cries. Then came the bull, by now slightly restive and uttering an occasional experimental bellow. Then came Lily. The point is that the procession proceeded at a walking pace.

I must put you out of your misery. No one was actually gored or tossed. Our friend Rudd, the athletic manager of the farm, boldly answered the pathetic cries, and tricked the bull into letting himself be locked up.

This little story is so liberally laced with morals that I will not commit the solecism of pointing any. I merely wish to point out that on my passage through the village that evening I was informed that:

(a) There was at that moment a bull in my garden;
(b) There had formerly been a cow in my garden;
(c) Kay had been chased through the village by a boar; and
(d) Kay had been seen pursuing a heifer with a spade.

I was naturally relieved to learn the true facts. Odd that no one mentioned a goat.

* * * *

If you want to buy a bloomer loaf you turn off the main street of the market town (at least, I do), and slip down a narrow hilly street that drops away to the tougher part of the town, where the pubs have chuckers-out.

These bloomer loaves are long, crusty, golden things that actually improve with keeping. Even when four days old and as tough as leather they still taste like bread. They are nothing like that brittle French stuff, except, slightly, in appearance.

When in town I never miss buying a couple. I have been looking for what I call a good loaf for years. A good loaf, like a good philosophy, is one that you enjoy, and to hell with dietetics and expert opinion.

There are other good reasons for visiting this particular little pastry-cook's. Sometimes, if your luck's in, you see the visiting gypsies there. It seems to be their favourite baker's too.

The other day there was quite a party of them, including one uninhibited girl who had got on the wrong side of the counter and was being shoo'd out by one of the charming if slightly inhibited women who serve there, wearing starched caps midway in shape between a bishop's lid and a Nippy's. She just wanted to look round, the gypsy said.

The gypsy women seem to be in a transitional stage. Well, all gypsies are. In a generation or less they will be urban. These were hippy, bosomy women of tremendous character and vitality.

They were all dressed for town in light grey suits nipped in hard at the waist. The older ones wore high boots and glossy straw hats, the younger ones high-heeled shoes and lovely, silly little wispy hats perched on top of their heads. Not a shawl among them.

They had leather-brown faces and tight little brown ringlets and big gold earrings, and their teeth and eyes flashed as they chattered, and they exuded a great wave of vitality and made everyone else look and feel enervated and self-conscious.

I gathered that they were buying a cake, but whether for a wedding or a birthday I couldn't be sure. The main thing was that it must look immensely glamorous, in a citified way. No doubt the pastry-cook's art represents the extreme of sophistication if you do all your cooking over a fire of twigs.

They couldn't agree whether to take a pink cake or a yellow one and in the end they took them both. I would have given a month of television to be at that party, though just to think of all that icing makes my teeth ache.

When they had gone it suddenly seemed as quiet as Sunday.

I bought my bread, saying clearly and distinctly, 'Two small bloomer loaves, please.' I have to rehearse this little speech every time and it bothers me a bit.

I know for sure that if I relax my concentration for a moment, the old subconscious will take over and I shall see the kind lady's face change and hear a deathly hush fall over the shop. And I shall know that means I've gone and asked for a small pair of bloomers, please.

5

Summer

When I stopped to give the horses their expected gift of biscuits, a full hundred yards from the river bridge, I could see swallows and swifts swooping down to the surface of the water and rising again in graceful shallow arcs. Then I knew that the Mayfly hatch was in full swing.

The surface was wimpled with the rings of rising fish and hatching flies, breaking through to the light of day in the moment of liberation which is, for so many of them, also the moment of doom.

I sat down at the river's edge to watch the drama in which Mayflies, birds, and fishes all take part. All the fishes in the stream and all the birds that lived along its banks were alerted to the occasion. The river is never so electrically alive as during this deeply moving festival of slaughter and fulfilment, triumph and disaster.

As each Mayfly struggled up through the surface film it sat for some moments on the skin of water, shaking out its wings, drying them and gathering strength and purpose to take flight. All the time it was being carried remorsely downstream by the current.

Some were sucked down by waiting trout before they had floated many feet. Some were picked off the surface by swooping birds. Some struggled up into the air only to be snapped in a bird's beak. Some lucky ones, marked out by Fate to fulfil their destiny, flew staggering away to alight in tall bushes beside the stream.

I knew what was to come and what had gone before. Two years ago the female Mayfly had laid her eggs on the ever-changing surface of this stream. They had drifted down to the bottom. In a dark burrow in the river's bed the larvae had lived through two whole seasons.

Then the mysterious urge had come upon those inch-long, dull, unhandsome grubs. With desperate energy they had forced their way up from the silt to the surface, obeying a command implanted in them, the deep primal imperative which none can disregard.

Now for a day, or two, or three, the survivors, miraculously changed first from grub to fly, then from dull fly to brilliant diaphanous fly, would rest and dance in the glitter of the light. They would not eat, for they had no mouths.

Eventually males and females would meet in the ritual mating dance. For the males, mating is the end of the story; he flies away to die unnoticed. But the female, now in her height of glory, translucent and beautiful, would dip down with azure wings brilliantly beating to the surface of the stream which bore her, and seeming to kiss the water, she would lay her eggs and make sure of the life to come, beyond the individual. Then she would sink down and with a final tremor spread her wings on the water, one again in death with the stream that made and claimed her.

*   *   *   *

Though it is embowered in green, densely draped in the richest foliage of the year, our little world yearns for the sun. Persistent dry winds chafe the surface of the soil, and it grows paler. We like to see it darkly gleaming. The great inverted bowl of sky is the colour and weight of lead.

Yet with or without the sun, this is indubitably summer. Last night a swallow arrived, pitching down on the ridge of the bent old roof, then swerving down to cling to the clothes-line. He gave the barn swallow's twittering cry, several times, and then he rose again and displayed his lyre-shaped tail and creamy-beige belly as he flew off to the farm buildings. Perhaps he had mistaken the old cottage for a barn.

How far had he flown, against contrary airs, over the great tilled plain of Continental Europe, over hills and seas and revolutions? He had seen innumerable rivers that I long to see again, and at the end of his prodigious odyssey he pitched down on our ancient roof. Noble and beautiful birds, so brave and so good for the heart, stay with us this summer.

The home-keeping, unadventurous little birds are busy by my window. My desk is placed close up at a beetle-browed casement under the overhang of a tile-hung wall, and there rises before it a dense tall hedge. So my thoughts cannot stray very far.

Hedge sparrows live in this dense mixed wall of thorn and ivy and ash, and in snug crevices in the tile-hung wall of the cottage, house sparrows are bringing up their families. About this window there is a continual coming and going of small, modest, earth-coloured birds.

The hedge sparrows are comparatively trim and elegant,

the house sparrows are mousey, fluffed-out, untidy little things with no pretensions to good looks. No matter. Their vivacious communities keep me company on the loneliest day.

In these arid times, waiting for rain as well as sun, we water the seedlings and the frailer growths when evening comes. It is a haphazard process, which grows upon you, once you start, like eating a bag of mixed sweets.

Just a drop for the tagetes, you say, having noticed their tiny bifurcated shoots. Then it is just a drop for the alyssum along the border, just a drop for the new aubretia on the new stone wall, just a drop for the sweet peas.

So it goes on, can after can. You might just as well have run out the hose to begin with. In the end you are far from complacent, indeed you are conscious of how ineffective a rainmaker you are. But there is nothing in the catalogue of horticultural odd jobs so soothing and godlike as watering. Once you have started you cannot stop. It is a process which ministers wonderfully to your self-esteem.

Especially to someone who, like me, feels a deep mystical affinity with water, the mysterious element in which we all had our remote origin. To be bestowing the life-giving stuff on organisms which are parched for it is one of the deepest, and cheapest, of pleasures.

Then the thrush who sings alone, every evening at dusk, high in the walnut tree, opens his heart. The grey day closes on his song of undiluted ecstasy.

*   *   *   *

Pablo the cat walked delicately through the daisies. He did not seem to see them but he never trod on them. He put his feet down in the grass more beautifully than a dancer. Yet they went down firm.

Pablo was young. He was living his first summer. He knew some quiet old cats but he did not connect them with a cat's proper life. He had a short-haired white coat and a tabby mask and cap. His strong tapering tail was tabby and there were three tabby medallions on his back, like over-lapping pennies. He had a face like a lynx and he walked like a tiger.

He loved two people, in his way, and recognized three or four human friends. To all that flew or fluttered or crawled or skipped or crept along on four little legs he was implacably opposed. But his many enmities did not make him unhappy.

Pablo stepped off the grass on to a flower bed and stopped dead. He pressed his paws down and felt the dry sun-warmed soil on his pink pads. He stood for a moment feeling the dusty soil and then he flung himself down and rolled in it, closing his eyes. He rolled three times and sighed deeply and lay still. Under the miniature tree which was a hydrangea he slept in the sun for a moment of eternity.

When Pablo opened his eyes the sun had not moved round the woody stem, but he had lost consciousness and taken some of its power into himself during his momentary trance. When he opened his eyes the world was new.

He lay for a moment watching a butterfly fluttering about a deep red paeony, two yards from his hydrangea tree. It was a common Cabbage White, though, of course, neither the butterfly nor the cat knew that.

Pablo rolled over imperceptibly until he was crouched on all fours. He began to edge forward until he was almost directly beneath the butterfly.

He gathered his powers until he was quivering like a taut spring and he leaped vertically in the air.

The butterfly flapped away silently and Pablo turned in the air, reaching for it. He came down with a crash in the foliage of the paeony.

For a moment Pablo stood still, blinking in the sun. Then he began to chew a long blade of couch grass which the hoe had missed.

A Cottage Idyll

He boxed it like a punch ball and then he seized it with both paws, sitting up like a squirrel, and he chewed it down to the stalk.

Pablo washed his face briefly and strolled off down the broad walk of grass. As he went he leaped in the air after insects too small for the human watcher's eye to see.

Skipping and leaping the little cat went down the long path, and he vanished into the dense hedge of beech and yew and thorn, and the sun shone on a garden that suddenly seemed empty.

* * * *

The last of the Dragons sailed away, hull-down and hell-bent for the island's lee. Dragons, which are racing yachts, are built for speed, and like salmon and swallows they are beautiful. When a thing built for speed is inhabited only by its own resident spirit, that is a form of perfection. When a thing built for speed is inhabited by an alien, a driver or pilot, then its beauty may be flawed. But drivers and pilots may be beautiful too. Sometimes they partake of the spirit of the thing they ride.

But some people do not believe in resident spirits. For this loss there is no known remedy.

When the Dragons left the scene I began to feel the loneliness of the sea. This is one of the prime ingredients in the pleasure of sailing, and especially of sailing single-handed. There was now only a big ketch tacking across the tide, and a few fishermen running for home with their engines fussing and fuming. Then the ketch too went about and ran for harbour, and by the time I had trimmed my sails and lit the stove they had all disappeared. They were all servants or slaves of the haven-gifted tide, as I had been many times. But this day by a golden chance I was free of that harbour's inexorable conditions. I was free to stay outside, if I chose, and I chose. Most times I too had to run in over the bar before the ebbing water slammed the harbour shut.

More than once I had been last in the race to beat the tide, a frightened fugitive from the ocean. But today I had the means to stay outside, I had the treasure of time. And I meant to squander it. So in a few minutes, as it seemed, I was left alone on the sea.

I do not know how it is with other spare-time sailors, but to me those first few minutes when you realize that you have burned your bridges and you cannot get back into harbour for the term of a tide, and you are alone on the sea – those are moments of great intensity, when you worry and experience fear, but also you experience exhilaration. From this moment onwards it does not greatly matter if you sail out for a year, or sail back to port on the next tide: the intensity of the experience is a question of quality, and quantity does not affect it greatly. Prolongation does not profoundly or radically affect it. It is pure. You are on your own and you don't really know for sure whether you are in your right mind. This subtle mingling of emotions is at the root of the joy. There is no other way, at least there is no other way known to me, of enjoying this particular emotion. It cannot be counterfeited or apprehended vicariously. To experience it, you have to cast off.

To a man on the sea, in a small boat of which he is only nominally the master, the wind is rarely quite right. When it falls light you set up a clamour for more, you make a bold tut-tut and to-do about it; but when it gets up you pray most earnestly for less. When you have the perfect breeze which lets you run free at a slightest angle of heel, sailing full-and-by and fast enough to make the purling water sing along the hull, with the helm alive under your hand and the sails full and the sheets taut, why, then you know perfection, and you also know very vividly and inescapably that it cannot last.

But this I find is the mysterious sauce of contentment, this knowledge within you that you are experiencing a perfection that cannot last. I think it sharpens your perceptions. Rose growers know it too. I think it is part and parcel of the pleasure of men who tend turf. I tend turf and I grow roses and sometimes I sail a small boat on the sea and I am familiar with this ephemeral essence of perfection. The pleasure is mixed up in the impermanence.

A little cruise is just like life. If you are lucky, a little sail such as a man may make in a boat like mine contains a bit of everything you need. Moments of fear, moments of exhilaration, singing moments of perception, spells of relaxation, toil and change. It may end at any moment, in disaster. It may make a fool of you, or it may make you feel momentarily rather clever and even rather good. It will assuredly show you to yourself. Nearly all the problems of life on land are present on the sea, and some are magnified; but on the sea it is possible to escape for a time from the congestion and contagion of the world. All the privacy you can want is to be had on the ocean.

One does not want it all the time but when it is needed it is needed badly.

I brooded for a while over the compass and considered the set of the tidal stream, and the steady wind, and I set my course. I thought of the racing Dragons riding now at their moorings, their gallant crews drinking cocktails or changing for dinner. They too were enjoying their lives, in their own way. As I stood out from the land it began to grow dark. I checked that the lamps had plenty of oil and lit them and hung them in the shrouds. With the wind as it was she would just steer herself, at any rate for short periods; the tiller moved gently from side to side as she slid through the water. Everything was just right, and I was just sufficiently apprehensive to enjoy it to the full. I ate some bread and a little cheese, and when the kettle boiled I made a mug of tea. And I laced it with whisky. I washed up; you have to stick rigidly to domestic routine or the boat is all huggermugger in no time. I pulled on my oilskin jacket and rolled a cigarette and I settled down at the helm.

The turf which I had left close-cropped was springing as I sailed, the rose buds were bulging; when I got back home everything would be different yet the same. It would be a wonderful moment to get back home. But now was now.

*   *   *   *

At the tail of the weir the stream divides and flows with a careless grace and music on either side of a long island shaped like an egg. On this island the ruins of the priory glow golden in flashes of sunlight and fade again to grey as storm clouds rush across the sky.

When I feel out of love with the contemporary scene I like to come and fish here, where the monks fished before me. Everything has changed since the monks built their priory. You can see factory chimneys on the far skyline, and hear, not from afar, the nervous music of engines. The woods have dwindled and the very fields have changed. The old walls are down to a few commanding fragments of weathered stone. But still the fish flash unchanged in the pearly water of the stream as they flashed all those centuries ago.

The perch and pike have not changed, the roach and dace and chub are identical, and the trout, though infinitely fewer, still carry the blood-red spots on their dappled flanks and still live out their mysterious lives with incomparable dash and verve.

A growing sense of the continuity of life pervades you when you sit here fishing, at the tail of the island where the streams converge. Shrewd they were, the old monks who built their home on an island. Though they lived by an ideal – the most vaulting and lofty ideal imaginable – yet they were practical men, and men of many parts.

There was nothing other-worldly in their approach to this world. They were farmers and weavers, brewers and gardeners, butchers and bakers, millers and joiners, apothecaries and smiths, artisans and artists. They were all those things and they were anglers too. So they chose a site which gave their home a living moat all round it. A moat for security and for food.

Sometimes when you sit drowsing in the sun where the angler monks sat – how many thousands of times, how many centuries ago? – you fancy that you can hear again the solemn bell tolling from the tower that is humbled, hear again the swish of monkish habits and the sonorous dignity of Latin prayer.

No doubt the fishing was better in their day. Whether the life was better, I do not know. Perhaps it was idyllic and simple. Perhaps it was brutal, savage and superstitious. But what is it now? At least there were these oases of cultivation and self-sufficient peace.

Some scholars hold that all that was worth preserving was preserved, through the Dark Ages, by the monks. Some say that they were merely escapists, self-indulgent and corrupt. I daresay the truth lies somewhere in between. However that may be, the sense of the past is strong as you sit fishing at the tail of the island, in the shadow of the grey stone. The creel grows heavy and the heart grows light, and the sun goes down behind the shattered walls.

* * * *

When the sun is high and mighty and the sky is really azure – it may not happen a score of times in an English year – then you realize how much the beauty of England depends on the soft customary English light.

The tall elms that ring us round have lost the brilliance and subtlety of their colours. Their tender lights are put out by the strong sun; they seem almost grey. Landscape shimmers and dances and is drowned in a flood of light.

It is a beauty of a kind, a kind we are not accustomed to. The magnificent brassy flamboyance of a hot afternoon is glorious only because it is rather rare. I think I might hate it if it were customary. It did not breed the tough, tender-hearted, tranquil, supple, stubborn, easy-going, eccentric, individual English. They were bred on land that squelched. But it is wonderful while it lasts.

To get the colour values true, now, you have to shorten your view, forsaking the long-shot of landscape for the close-up. And this is just as well, for in the garden the stage is set for the entrance of the star.

The English garden is a play or rather a pageant. First comes the New Year flower, the demure and modest aconite: a walking-on part in an empty theatre. Snowdrops and crocuses make a brief bow while the audience settles down, rustling and complaining, and the orchestra tunes up.

Spring breaks loose in a fanfare with polyanthuses and daffodils.

Now the stage fills with important and resplendent figures that belong to summer. Assured and polished, self-sufficing and almost too well-groomed, tulips come on like a chorus of unapproachable beauties, and the other side of the stage fills up with dressy wallflowers, vivid and jolly and much more fun to know.

And the blue flowers burst in, juveniles all; forget-me-nots and bluebells multiplying by a sort of magic. The fat beaming buttercups called trollius or globe flower take their places down the wings with the fat dowdy daisies that I love so well, the pyrethrums.

Grandeur builds up with the first staggering spires of the lupins, the composed and almost haughty irises, the power of paeonies, the exoticism of azaleas.

We are ready for the star. The setting, which began all brown and slowly changed to green, is flooding with new colours.

The red may is out, lilacs are bursting in bunches of white and purple, laburnum dripping fronds of buttery gold, honeysuckle and guelder rose creaming into colour. You can see the pinks starting to flush into flower. It is the final cue. You must keep your eye on the stage.

One morning quite soon, after just an ordinary night with nothing special happening, no shooting star nor sign in heaven, you will walk out to find a rose in bloom.

*   *   *   *

Now the nights are almost as short as they will ever be. I have suffered as much as I have enjoyed in the night and I love the merciful dawns of summer.

Although in many respects I am a shockingly inconsistent man, I have a bedtime habit which is pretty well invariable. For more than a quarter of a century I have always tried to read a little history or poetry before going to sleep. History settles the mind as soda settles the stomach. It sends me off into reveries about the land I live in and love. It takes the mind off its small nagging personal preoccupations. When you see yourself against the backcloth of history your successes seem as endurable as your failures.

Of course, there is a danger in living too much in the past; but possibly there is a greater danger in living exclusively in the present or wishfully in the future. A sense of continuity, of rootedness in an endless process of ancestry, is not too bad a thing.

The room in which I read is congenial to this odd pursuit. It is a box of beams roughly filled in with white-washed bricks. The bricks were hand-fired of local clay in a kiln now long disused, lost to sight, down a green lane which rarely feels a footstep, save my own.

But the great rough oaken beams came from afar, and it is a marvel to me still how they come to be here, in this hamlet that shelters under the shoulder of the Downs. For they were the ribs of ships that sailed before the first *Mayflower*. Were they taken from wrecks washed ashore in the innumerable creeks of the tide-angry Channel? Or from shipwrights whose sheds and slipways have dotted the wooded inlets of Hampshire and Sussex for centuries, and still stand? No one knows for sure. But they must have come up from the seaways and over the Downs.

They were roughly worked with crude hand tools. They were hacked into shape with axe and adze. They are as hard as iron, as black as coal. It is a wonderful thought: perhaps they were growing in the New Forest before Rufus rode out to his death?

Sometimes in the silence of a summer night you can hear exactly the same sounds that your predecessor heard, lying wakeful in the same room hundreds of years ago, when it was fine and new. When all man's traffic has gone by, and not a wheel turns, you can hear the owl; and sometimes, if your luck holds, the fox and the nightingale.

You realize that in the scale of history the old cottage is very new. Fox and owl and nightingale had the Saxon night to themselves, and the Roman night, and the Celtic night, and all the long dark night before human history began. Nightingale, owl, and fox have seen history through and it has not changed them. But men are changed by what they do. A wind comes wandering up from the sea, a green wind blowing, and the last thing you hear before you fall asleep is the immemorial conversation of the elms.

*   *   *   *

What is going on all around me as I sit here under the young willow tree at midsummer? Life is going on. The life which some hasty people call simple. It is a very complex business indeed, this simple life. It has uncountable facets and angles and complications. I shall never get to the bottom of it.

The life of this young willow tree, now: it is going forward triumphantly, more splendid by far than an army with banners. Already, in its fourth year here, there is that sudden thickening at the base of the trunk which means that it is ready to grow. The roots have been taking hold, below ground, through several summers, fighting the first great battle in a tree's life. Now I know that under the turf on which I sit a massive root system has established its right to live on its own terms. Now there is a surplus of energy made available and the trunk suddenly thickens, right where it emerges from the turf. In the next three years our little tree will race away, shooting up, spreading out, growing gloriously to its fulfilment. This, surely, is far from simple. This is the victory of a tree's life. It is never by any means certain until it is won.

There is another little tree growing in the rough grass, hardly taller than the grass itself. This is our only oak. The great writer Henry Williamson gave it to me, as a token of friendship. I carried it 200 miles from its birthplace high above the estuary of the Twin Rivers, Taw and Torridge: the land of *Tarka the Otter*. It seems to have taken kindly to us, the little friendship oak. We are looking after its life as well as we can. The life of the infant oak, then, that is going on. What else?

There is no statistician, no electronic computer, no robot brain in the wide world capable of calculating the separate lives now going forward all around me. I am content because I do not wish to injure a single one of them. Many will come to a tragic end, but not at my hand.

The blackbird calling to his mate from the old Blenheim apple tree is perfectly poised in his one particular position in the dazzling scheme of interlocking lives that now surge forward to their fulfilment on the tide of summer.

There are two more lives going forward here. There is the life of the garden as a whole. A garden is the sum of innumerable separate but related lives. People like us, who cannot paint pictures or write poems or compose music, we can have a shot at making a garden. In a garden everything dies but the garden's life goes on. It is the image of immortality, and the matrix of community.

Finally there is the life of a marriage. This too goes on. Shorter than the life of a tree, more precarious than the life of a bird: the vital human relationship that is really the one thing worth getting right, the source of all joy and peace.

*   *   *   *

The injured swan caught the glint of water as she flew over the hidden valley. It was no more than a glimpse, for tall trees grow down steep banks to the water's edge, and the lake is very small.

Wheeling painfully, the swan banked to make a circuit. But she had come too far already. Nobody knows how far, or what drove her. But too far. She side-slipped out of the sky, lurching and staggering, suddenly graceless and clumsy. They found her in a garden, lying still, as hurt things do.

When she was well again they took her down to the lake. So she made it after all. She would be company, they thought – kind people – for the cob that swam up and down, up and down, unapproachable in his loneliness since brutal young soldiers strangled his mate, for fun.

But it was not a love match at first sight. (Does that ever happen, except in the human world?) Again and again, neck and wings outstretched, menacing, the cob drove her into the steep woods. She bore his malice meekly. It was as if she knew she must wait patiently. As if she knew that she had come home. In the end one instinct conquered another, and the cob accepted her.

Last year there was a flotilla of fluffy cygnets on the lake. The trout fishers damned them all heartily – save a few who were wise enough to feel well rewarded by the sight. The village children who ran squealing to bathe, the motorists who brought their picnic meals to the valley, were pleased. They saw the swan as a tasteful afterthought, a decorative finishing touch to an idyllic scene. But whether it is safe to think of Nature as tasteful or idyllic, I could not be sure.

This year there will be no brood of babies. They found the cob dead, his head crushed. There are no inquests or trials in the natural world. The facts are final.

The swan swims up and down the lake, and pauses, like a toy swan on a mirror. To the picknickers, the fishers, and the children, the swan is just a swan. She cannot tell her story. She is mute.

But you can watch, and guess, and wonder. And be sure there is a change coming.

Now the endless slow progress up and down the lake is often interrupted. The swan is preening again, tidying herself.

And there is a new sound in the valley. Several times a day, with a great beating of pinions, she launches herself into the air. She does not fly far, but she is practising her take-off. It is hard to fly out of the hidden valley.

Each time I go down to the lake I expect her to be gone. It will be at least the third time she has tried to find the life a swan needs, like any living creature. A place to call home, your own kind around you, and a bit of peace and quiet, in a swan's way.

I don't suppose she really remembers. Very likely I know more of her past than she does.

I wish I knew her future. I wish I could be lucky and see her start off on her new life, wheeling over the tall trees and heading . . . where?

*　　*　　*　　*

At the appointed hour the sea swelled in the Channel. In all the creeks and inlets of the Channel coast the transfiguring tide came dead on time. It stole up to Itchenor. Over the mudflats where at 4 a.m. a man had dug ragworms – a man alone and happy in the wide salt emptiness – over the mudflats the sea brimmed silently.

Now the ragworms writhed in an old iron dipper under a thwart of the dinghy, and the dinghy pulled at its painter as the

tide tugged. The man who had owned the empty estuary at
4 a.m. ate breakfast aboard a little old motor cruiser and awaited
his friends.

They drove south through a misty morning, through Mid-
hurst and Lavant and rose-embowered Chichester, and down
narrow lanes past cottages garlanded with roses, and so to the
salt creek.

Then the dinghy put out from the cruiser *Nidea* to pick them
up. *Nidea* that had made the immortal voyage to Dunkirk, and
now, like an old horse put out to grass, dreamed away the tides
in peace.

The newcomers were welcomed aboard, and instantly, in
their imagination, land-lubberliness fell away, and they were
sailors. It is true that they got in the way and said the wrong
things and in their extreme innocence were heard to call a warp
a rope. But all was forgiven, for their hosts knew that they were
tasting salt on their lips and dreaming moon-mad dreams. At
such a time, when the planks tremble beneath your hand and
the slapping salt water speaks in your secret heart, a landlubber
is above himself.

Soon enough the brief voyage was over and the mooring
secured. But they were still afloat, two in the dinghy and the
others on the parent ship, and all isolated by eternities from the
humdrum life ashore. On the far shore men like midgets moved
about other occupations, as remote as men in Mars. The tide
made in, the mudflats vanished, a pair of nesting herons circled,
and wild duck flew over.

And fish came in with the tide, the gallant gleaming bass
and the flat-footed flounder. Merrily the reels sang, and rods
bend in fluent curves. Then suddenly there was no more motion
and the boats hung poised at the top of the tide like cars on the
Big Wheel at a fair. For a hushed moment it was slack water,
the precarious equilibrium of high tide. Then the pendulum
began to swing again, the sea began to slip out of the estuary,

birds came down to the mudflats with cries of joy, and the sea fish departed.

The landlubbers were put ashore, still drunk with salt water and unsteady from the intoxication of their dreams. They carried fish home, to the stable tideless haven of the bonfire and the hoe. Now it was a time for joking: and, looking back, it had been a day of jokes, quiet harmless leg-pulling and a little mild horseplay.

So they joked the evening away and fried the fish with chips from their own potatoes, newly dug. And the women said now that was something *like* fishing, when you brought home recognizable sea fish, fish that actually went with chips.

'Frying tonight!' said Kay gaily: and the hot fat hissed in the pan.

But to one landlubber at least there was something behind the joke that was splendid and serene. He fell asleep with the moon on his face, and dreamed of a life as salty and rhythmic as the tide.

*   *   *   *

Meg was nothing to look at, but like most mothers she did all the work. Meg tended to wear rusty tones of brown and grey and sometimes she looked frankly tatty. But her eye was always bright.

It was also always on the main chance. Well, when you have a family to raise and a work-shy husband who prefers hanging around on the corner, showing off, you have to keep an eye on the main chance. It was all the old man could do to keep himself. Meg scratched a living for the rest of them from the little plot. It wasn't very fertile, and she did a bit of begging on the side.

They let her beg. The young 'uns were a rowdy lot and the old man was vanity itself. He fancied himself as a vocalist and he was always letting rip to anybody who would listen. Meg soon got quite brazen about the begging she had to do. She would come right in and openly beg food for the nippers.

Now why should anybody want to attack a hard-working mother like Meg? It will always be a mystery. Anyway, one morning she was gone. Meg was never a quitter. She didn't walk out on them. There is no doubt she was murdered.

Now the old man had to face the facts of family life. To do him justice, he faced them manfully. The widower in black soon became a familiar figure, working the small-holding and feeding the family. He grew less spry but he was always on the job. The kids were growing up fast. Soon there was only one left at home. But between this one and the widower there seemed a special bond.

The kid grew at a great rate and soon he was almost as big as his dad. But still the widower slaved to feed him, and he was as tender to that great rowdy oaf as any mother could be. Last time I saw the widower he touched me for a bit of bread and cheese. I crept to the corner after him just to see what happened. Sure enough, there was the great bullying oaf of a son waiting with his beak wide open, and the old blackbird popped the food into it and watched it go down with what I can only call a touch of paternal pride.

*   *   *   *

This man was forty-six, which he felt to be a pretty dodgy age, and he was standing by his kitchen window grilling bacon for a sandwich and waiting for a miracle. It did not occur to him at the time that everything he saw through his kitchen window was miraculous, and nothing more miraculous than the fact that he was there to see it. That thought came to him later. He was a slow thinker at the best of times, and now he was thinking about grilling bacon, which is pretty near a full-time job.

But with half his attention he saw the young willows streaming in the West wind, the roses coming in their glory, the long

wigwam of bean poles up again and glistening in the rain, and
beyond all the standing wall of sentinel elms, dark against a
sky in which the clouds were like mountains moving. An old
Welsh saying came back to him, which he had heard from his
friend Tom Jones, the philosophical fisherman:

If you want to be happy for a day – get drunk.
If you want to be happy for six months – kill a pig.
If you want to be happy for a year – get married.
If you want to be happy for a lifetime – make a garden.

Well, he thought, I've tried them all. But he wasn't sure that
he agreed with that time-scale. Beer and bacon, the hop and the
hog, had always been comforters; not just for a day, not just for
six months. This man was very partial to the pig, the beast which
stood between him and the aberration of vegetarianism. He was
by way of being a bacon specialist. There was no flesh he liked
better. Left to himself he would practically live on the stuff. Like
most bacon fanciers, he liked it crisp and he liked to cook it
himself, at odd times of the day.

As for getting married . . . Suddenly it came to him that he
had been married exactly half his life, almost to the day. At
once this struck him as a miraculous thing in itself, against
all likelihood and reason. When he was young no one who knew
him would have taken a bet on his chances of living that
long, much less maintaining a marriage, which is no laughing matter. But then again . . . If it isn't a laughing matter,
what is it? Perhaps that's why it had lasted: it was a laughing
matter.

He was beginning to get deep in thought, which is very bad
for him. Then as he gazed through the kitchen window he saw
a little procession come into view. A small, slim figure wearing
an absurd but fetching duffel coat against the driving rain, with
a bright silk scarf over her red hair, which is starting to go paler.
And behind, at regular intervals, two little coats, keeping

station on their mistress, plodding through the rain towards the kitchen door.

Yes, the man thought, it certainly is a laughing matter, and quite probably a miracle into the bargain. He dipped a slice of bread in the fat and laid the crisp rasher on it and he went to the open door to greet his friends.

*   *   *   *

There was no panic when Kay discovered, about ten minutes before lunchtime, that there wasn't enough parsley in the entire half-acre to make a drop of parsley sauce. The old clump was virtually finished, the newly sown parsley was only just showing through the fine dark tilth.

A slight technical hitch, that's all. When you live in the country among good neighbours you don't worry about a slight technical hitch. Kay strolled unconcernedly through the gap in the hedge to beg a bit of parsley from our neighbour, Lily. She was gone rather a long time, I thought, but I put it down to the incurable talkativeness of women. When she returned she was smiling, and carrying just about the smallest possible amount of parsley that would make a drop of sauce.

Lily, too, happened to have just dug up her old clump, and her newly sown stuff wasn't even showing above ground yet. They had managed to grub up a few fragments from between the bricks bordering the path. So there it was – the best part of an acre of ground and not a handful of parsley to be had from it. Bad management, of course. Needless to say, there was any amount of mint. There was sage in abundance, and a plenitude of chives. There was thyme and marjoram, both Pot and Golden. But no parsley.

Now I am always on the point of taking over the management of the Herb Garden. So far it exists only as a convenient fiction in our minds. It is a terminological abstraction, not a palpable entity. True, if you search diligently you can find examples of most herbs – excepting, parsley, of course – but you find them scattered about in odd corners, mute testimony to a happy-go-lucky approach to gardening (if not to life itself).

My grandiose plan is to assemble in one exquisite plot all the fragrant, beautiful and consoling herbs. I want to grow them all together in happy and appropriate neighbourliness. Many times I have drawn a little plan of this plot and it is very nearly as good as writing out a poem. Consider the names of the herbs, the disembodied essences:

Pennyroyal, hyssop, angelica, bergamot, fennel, balm. Rue, sorrel, marjoram, mint. Tarragon, thyme, chives, sage.

These names are not only poetry; they are history. Living history. There is continuity in these names, and a thousand years of true civilization. They link you directly with the England that Shakespeare knew. They survive, like badgers and birds, out of an older way of life into the new and tatty civilization of tins-and-telly.

One day I am going to compose this horticultural poem. No doubt we shall find ourselves short of parsley again, but we shall never be short of a sense of the past, which is perhaps the best sauce for the unpalatable present.

*   *   *   *

Pop hadn't finished putting up the bean poles before the birds were on to it. They don't miss a thing. I reckon our birds are getting more human every generation. I know that is a serious accusation to make, but they asked for it.

I wouldn't like to say what is happening to the evolutionary pattern in the bird world, but it makes you wonder. We have birds on the payroll here who would rather walk than fly. As for working for a living, the whole conception is out of date. Our lot are layabouts who expect a constantly rising standard of living dished up on a plate.

Well, I was saying, Pop rigged up the bean pole structure with his usual conscientious attention to detail. Some people just whack the poles into the ground and give a couple of turns of sisal and that's that. But not Kay's old man. Pop might be building the Forth Bridge. He reckons one pole to one bean shoot and a few over for extra structural stability. When you get down and crawl along inside this elongated wigwam, weeding, you are practically invisible. That's *before* the beans start climbing.

At the cross-pieces Pop really gets to work with the ball of string. I myself am one who uses a lot of string on a string job, but compared with Pop I am miserly. He really lashes out on the lashing. This year he used the biggest part of a ball of very nice soft-fibred garden string which I had incautiously left lying around. I forget just what it costs but it was approximately enough to buy a new set of rigging for a small yacht in the bad old days.

The birds were on this like a flash. Every year they regard the bean pole structure as a convenience specially erected for them. I mean convenience in every sense of the word. But this year, in addition to the usual valued perching and hide-out facilities, they had all this lovely soft garden string to go at. Relays of birds were at work before Pop got back indoors, pulling and heaving at the silky stuff and dashing off with it to line their nests.

We shall have to take a turn of wire round the cross-pieces after all.

Well, I hope they appreciate it. But having watched yet another generation growing up, I doubt if appreciation is a very conspicuous factor in a bird's make-up. It is quite an education to see a family of three enormous youngsters, looking actually bigger than their parents in their fluffy plumage, standing on the lawn squawking to be fed, with bread lying ankle-deep all round them. The poor old parent bird, working like a beaver and thin as a rake, has to pick the bread up and pop it into their huge gaping mouths.

A Cottage Idyll

I don't wonder that after a few weeks of this the parents kick the young ones out and snatch a bit of peace. If some human parents occasionally feel the same urge I shouldn't be at all surprised.

*   *   *   *

'Antirrhinum rust, drat it!' I distinctly caught the muttered oath as I sped along the edge of a curving border.

On the return trip I stopped the mower to investigate. My spouse was vigorously uprooting a number of antirrhinum plants. I was sorry to see it, for the antirrhinum is among my favourite flowers. Kay likes it rather less.

But I have had far too much experience of the delicate balance of power which governs all gardens to express a personal regret, which might have been misinterpreted as criticism. Instead, I gently commiserated with her on the loss of such fine plants.

'Oh, well,' Kay replied, 'gardeners have to have their excuses for failure, the same as anglers. My excuse is rust.'

I could see it. And once more I marvelled silently at the extreme tenacity and toughness of the green-fingered brigade. A gardener's life, so far as I can make out from the sidelines where I am content to remain an onlooker, is one long uncreasing war against innumerable enemies. Rust, virus, bacteria and vermin. Greenfly, blackfly, boll weevil, mole, jay, finch. Not to mention the weather.

But it is not only the natural foes against whom gardeners fight their endless battle. Human advisers are still more sinister. Suddenly it came back to me. I remembered the long war of attrition between Kay and our first part-time gardener, an old chap of matchless cunning and resource named Pete. Pete was the original cause, I think, of Kay's turning ever so slightly anti-antirrhinum. Pete was rabidly anti-aster and almost hysterically pro-antirrhinum, while Kay wanted asters more than anything. Like all gardeners, Pete regarded the plot as his personal property and insisted on growing what *he* liked. Kay did get her asters, but only at the cost of having antirrhinums, too. They were still at odds about the proper proportion of asters to antirrhinums when the German bombs began to uproot both, with lofty impartiality.

There, I suspect, you have the root of Kay's indifference to the antirrhinum. I don't think she is really depressed about the rust.

That Pete had a mania for clipping and cutting and chopping. No tree or shrub was safe from him. He used to explain, with a wealth of technical jargon, that everything grew better if you cut it back hard. Maybe it does, but since Pete was slightly less than five feet tall I always wondered if his advice was entirely pure and disinterested. What he really wanted was to cut everything down to his own level. Under various cunning disguises that is, of course, a pretty widespread wish.

*   *   *   *

One fine morning when there were dew and cobwebs on the grass I was shaving at the bathroom window, which is a kind of dormer with deep bird-haunted eaves, and looking out over our half-acre.

There below me a slender little party with red-gold hair, wearing faded denims and a sky-blue jersey, was weeding among the coreopsis, and watching her closely but otherwise doing no work whatsoever was a stout little party wearing a heavy fur suit in black and white designed on the lines of a head waiter's rig.

As I watched this familiar sight I was suddenly struck by a thought. God save all here (I thought) but it's ten years I've been keeping that cat and twenty years I've been keeping that woman. Twenty years to the day. And here's me forgotten our wedding anniversary.

However, when you have a wife as good as mine you don't

need to panic about momentarily forgetting one anniversary (and when you don't have a good wife you might as well forget 'em all and be damned). So I came down and made my peace with the pair of them and they were both very gracious about it.

The stout fellow in full furry evening dress went so far as to roll on his back and utter that abrupt, deep, growling brown purr which has disconcerted more than one visitor who thought he knew all there was to know about cats.

Even so, I felt that it was up to me to make a handsome gesture. So I let it be known that anything either of them fancied was theirs for the asking, just to commemorate the day. It was understood that the obliging Badger would settle for a ceremonial dinner of anything in the flesh, fish or fowl line that we happened to be having. What is good enough for us had always been good enough for him. Kay, on the other hand, couldn't think of a single thing she wanted, except more hours to the day, which I wasn't in a position to supply.

But I slipped out and drove into the town, thanking my stars for a woman who is at her happiest pottering around the garden in denims with her hair like blown flame. That isn't the sort of woman who is always urging a man to make more and spend more and cut a dash.

I bought a luxurious little plate of china with a pattern of gold flowers on a lustrous background of deep crimson, the loving product of craftsman and artist, and I hung it on the white-washed wall just above the hearth. In the cool cavern of our ancient room it glowed like a jewel, and there it will hang, I hope, another twenty years or more, illuminating and reminding.

*   *   *   *

When I found that the water supply to the bedroom had failed, I knew that this was the crisis I had been subconsciously expecting ever since our relatives arrived. Things had been going too well. From Friday to Sunday afternoon nothing had happened to re-kindle our relatives' dormant but deep-rooted suspicion that, though practically middle-aged, we were not old enough to run a home of our own.

Now everyone was waking up from the Sunday afternoon snooze and wanting a refreshing rinse before we set off to run a critical eye over our local beauty spots. I kept the water failure dark as long as I could by locking myself in the bathroom and singing 'The Erl King' ('Who rides there so late, Through the night so w-i-l-d?') while I fiddled hopelessly with the taps and the cistern. From time to time people hammered on the door and asked if I were taking a bath. When I realized that I should have to climb into the loft to examine the tank I made a clean breast of it.

Invidious comparisons were at once drawn between modern urban plumbing and the makeshift arrangements of the country-side. I maintained a dignified composure and fetched the step-ladder.

We keep the step-ladder in a little cubbyhole off my study, with some of my fishing tackle, the spare electric lamp bulbs, and a bag of string. Manoeuvring the blessed thing out I got one foot of it trapped in my landing net. I got it free at the trifling cost of trapping my fingers twice and dropping the step-ladder on a bulb. I was then free to wheedle it round the six sharp corners that lay between me and the loft. I was in good form. I knocked almost nothing down and fetched very little paint off the door-frames.

It was so dark in the loft that I could hardly see the water tank, much less see inside it. I called for a torch, and someone wandered vaguely on to the porch, looking for I can't imagine what. I climbed down and fetched it myself.

Even with the torch I was not much wiser. The inside of the tank looked horrible, but at least it was full of water. So we decided that the trouble must be an airlock. I pushed and pulled at every bit of machinery I could see in the tank. It made awful sucking noises, but no water came out of the taps.

I rolled up my sleeve and reached down into the pipes that led out at the bottom of the tank. It was deeper than I thought and my sleeve became unrolled. I had used the torch to prop open the lid of the wooden box in which the water tank is enclosed. The torch slipped into the water and the lid fell on my head.

When I had changed my shirt I put my head in the wash-basin. Upside down, to try to break the airlock by sucking at the tap. I sucked until I was black in the face, but all I got was a gurgling noise and a mouthful of iron filings.

It was bitter, but I had to admit defeat. Everyone queued at the kitchen sink for a swill wearing expressions of extreme forbearance, while we tried to think whom we could 'phone for help. I 'phoned the waterworks first. The operator seemed ominously surprised when I asked for the number. When I got through a woman's voice said I should have to get on to The Company at Woking. I could not believe that The Company at Woking would want to hear from me in the middle of Sunday afternoon, so we tried to recall the name of the plumber who lived a few miles from our village. All we could remember for certain was that his name was Joe. Well, we thought, we might as well start out on our ride and call in the village to ask Tim Solly what Joe's other name was and where he lived. We roused Tim from his siesta. Yes, he could tell us Joe's name. It was Fred. And Fred was on the 'phone.

We went back home to 'phone Fred. Even before I unlocked the door I could hear running water. I dashed upstairs. We had left the taps on and the water supply had mysteriously returned. A pity someone had left the drain plug in the hole. When we had finished mopping up the bathroom it did not seem worth while going for a ride. It was raining anyway.

*   *   *   *

Summer

Wanted, a big old walnut tree, over 7 ft circumference

– Advt. in The Times

I was sitting right here by the window doing no harm to anybody, and precious little good, and this man comes stalking in a great hurry up to the front door.

'I'll take your walnut,' he cried without a 'Good morning'. 'I'll give you a good price.'

'Well, I said, 'I don't think we've *got* any that we want to sell. We've a fair bit of mahogany, if you're interested, and an old iron bedstead, but the only walnut I'd be glad to see the back of is the television set. And that's only veneer, I fancy.'

'No, no!' he cried impatiently. 'Not *that* sort of walnut! *This* is the walnut I'm after.' And he set off down the garden path again at a smart pace, with me behind him in my slippers. He was a quick little chap like a robin.

He rushed up to the old walnut tree in the gate and flung his arms round it as if he loved it. (Well, so do I.) He did a little dance round it and then he whipped out a tape measure and danced round it again.

'Just the size,' he cried happily. 'I'll take it away. You won't have no trouble. What did you say your name was? How about Wednesday?'

'Hold on,' I said. 'It isn't mine to sell, and I'm sure my landlord wouldn't sell it, and I wouldn't either. I like having it here.'

'Who's your landlord?' he asked, testily. 'I'll go and see him. It's a sin to leave a tree like that.'

'My landlord's abroad,' I said. Well, he often is, but at that moment he drove down the lane and past the cottage. He waved, and I waved back, thinking, well, perhaps if I live a good life I may be forgiven the innocent lie.

'Pity,' said the walnut collector. 'Just the right size and I'd take it away so you'd hardly know it'd been there.'

145

'Well,' I said, 'I'm sorry, but it's not for sale.'
'You must be rolling in money,' the man said.
'Rolling in it,' I said. May I be forgiven.
'Ah!' said the man, darkly.
'Ah, indeed,' said I. 'And think how we'd miss the nuts.'
'*Nuts?*' said the tree feller.
'Nuts,' said I.

* * * *

The rifle jumps very slightly when you fire, and you smell again the old smell of gunpowder and gun oil and blued steel and walnut. There is a flat wooden thwack and you know that at least you have hit the wooden board on which the target is pinned. That's something.

It is a long time since you fired a gun. But it all comes back. The ejector works with a satisfying clunk of well-fitted steel and as the spent cartridges spin out of the breech the spent years spin away too. But not enough of them.

It's no good beefing about it. The old eyes aren't what they were. You don't hold the gun so steady, either. All the same, you were pretty lethal. Your bullets have torn the card all round the bull. If it hadn't been a paper target, now . . .

Would you have killed a man? Easily. A rabbit? Yes. A squirrel? Very likely. A bird? Possibly: a fair sized bird.

Do you want to kill any of those creatures? Not really. Then what are you doing with that gun? Having fun. Letting off steam. Remembering. Guns, alas, are beautiful. You had forgotten just how beautiful.

You go in to dinner, in the calm old house set within its magic ring of grass and trees. The squirrel turns up before you have finished the first course. He puts his beautiful little hands on the step of the open french window and looks into the room. There are no crumbs down. They are all up on the bird table just outside. It takes him about twenty seconds to work it out. He turns and streaks up the pole and he swings himself on to the disc of cork where the food is laid out. He sits there eating bread and cheese and his bright dark eyes never leave you. His tail is against the setting sun like a translucent fan, beautiful gossamer red-brown-blue hairs arching out from the thick dark spine.

He rushes down and scuttles across the lawn and vanishes into the dark wall of trees. Birds that have been watching and waiting fly down to eat and you finish your dinner and the gun hangs on the wall, the beautiful gun, forgotten.

*   *   *   *

The summer holds. It is beautiful to walk abroad in the morning, and the evening is a song of praise.

At this time the heart turns away from gimmicks and gadgets. Gadgetry will come into its own again as an antidote to autumn, so lovely and so piercingly sad.

Then you feel the need to busy yourself in little constructive ploys. You fight off autumn's desolation and decay with busy hands.

But now it is the time to bask in the creation. From May until September, between the letting-out and the lighting of fires, you can live easily and calmly without novelty or distraction, in the luminous enchantment of the natural world.

Every summer I grow lazier. Everything I do I do more slowly. I lose all sense of haste. Curiously enough, though I grow increasingly aware of time's passing, yet by some strange paradox time is ceasing to have much meaning. The clock has less and less importance in my life.

Suffused with a sense of wonder and contentment, I am happy to include myself in the creation without badgering it with questions. And never a backward glance at the ambitions unrealized, the money unmade, the things undone that youth was set on doing.

Idle, easy-going, and perfectly unperplexed by the myriad

things I now know I shall never understand, I let myself drift with the tide of growth, on the wave of change. It is enough, abundantly enough, simply to be alive in the same creation as the things I love.

This is what cynics and eager-beavers and go-getters and all such neurotics call *vegetation*. They use the word like a whip.

Who can deny it? Not I. I vegetate unashamedly.

But then, the vegetable garden has its own beauty, and vegetables have an innocent way of life which will bear much watching. . . .

To feel the slow stir of sap, the warmth of sun and soil and the assuaging drench of rain. To come to ripeness in due season, crisp and fresh, wholesome and juicy . . . Not a bad cycle, from seed to sink.

After a holiday it takes a little time to settle back into the routine of humdrum daily life. But the pattern you made long ago sturdily asserts itself and every day takes hold of you a little more surely, until suddenly you realize that you are truly home again, the holiday adventure over, living the chosen life at the chosen pace.

I do not know which is the most sinister enemy of contentment – boredom or envy or slavery to the clock. All three are banished from the quiet timeless world of the happy idler who lingers in coppice and garden and by the bird-haunted water, no man's debtor, master and slave of none.

* * * *

Dry days and ripening fruits come together in a proper summer. The birds know this well. In the dog days they steal berries to assuage their thirst. And so do we. Not to assuage the physical dryness, which we quench in something else; but to slake the thirst perpetual for yesterday and the lost, dream-peopled groves of youth. The fleeting truant flavour of a golden age, the tang and tartness and bitter-sweet heyday of childhood, are locked in the ripening currant, the gooseberry flushed with pink. Merely to taste them, picked fresh and furtively in morning sunshine, is to re-live haunted summers of long ago. Tongue and nose have longer memories than the mind.

Since all I had I stole, I find it uncongenial now to guard my crops too meanly. There is no figure more unsympathetic than the poacher turned gamekeeper. Be that as it may, altruism is not allowed too free a run. I accede (though my heart is not in it) to the subtle and complex plans that are laid to frustrate raiders.

Last year we experimented with nets. I was not too sorry when they failed wholly in their intention. Draped over the glowing bushes they had a mean and minatory look, a hint of prison. Anyway, the birds soon solved the problem. Fat as butter, unflurried, and supremely knowing, they toddled demurely under the mesh and ate their fill at leisure. When I hurried out in the mornings, a figure absurdly menacing, they toddled quietly out again and took to flight, with a mocking froosh of wings.

This year we settled for those bright metallic strips which flash like heliographs and crackle loudly in the breeze. We hung them along the top wire of a structure which I built this spring, only a degree less elaborate than Brooklyn Bridge, to discipline the lolling raspberries and the swarming, uncouth community of loganberries. They are as efficient as gunfire. The birds hated them and stayed away. I hated them too, flashing and banging away like a funfair in the garden.

The situation resolved itself, as most will, if you give them time. Whenever the flashing strips got tangled up, and were still, I kept forgetting to do a job I had not got my heart in, and gradually the birds crept back.

And not only the birds. My household, doubled by the arrival of venerable in-laws, proves more knavish than the birds. I notice that everybody, when caught in the act, explains it by saying: 'It was just falling off,' or some such transparent fib.

A Cottage Idyll

No one is deluded. Conscientiously I provide water for the birds and cider for the humankind. Both seem acceptable. But still the raiders take their toll of the forbidden fruits, and summer dozes in its timeless trance.

* * * *

One curious by-product of a hot summer is that I find myself committed (in principle) to a reorganization of the heating system of our cottage. I have stood out against it for years; but a hot summer has done what five winters could not. There is nothing wrong with the heating system, really. It is all too effective. What I am asked to invest in would be more accurately described as a de-heating system.

Our kitchen faces slightly west of south. It used to be a sort of lean-to at the back of the cottage. The steeply raked roof, supported on pillars, projected far beyond the back wall and made a useful shelter for logs and bicycles and the dog kennel and the robin's nest. A genius before our time built in three walls and made it into an additional room. Judging by the congregation to be found at all sorts of hours sitting around speaking no evil and drinking tea or stout or wine, it is considered the most attractive room in the house.

It is by no means one of those super glossy hygienic galleys untouched by human hand which you see in the smooth magazines, but it does possess distinct character and a sort of wry, rough charm. It is lighted by a long lattice window that runs most of the length of the south wall: under its white-tiled sill the working units are arranged in a rather deceptively efficient looking line: cooker, fridge, sink, draining boards, cupboards and so on. The back door is also largely of glass.

There is room for some furniture: it is not merely a machine for cooking in. We painted plain wooden chairs and stool cream, and upholstered the important parts in scarlet leather pinned down by dome-headed brass nails. There is an ancient oak dining table which, although too heavy to move and apparently as solid as granite, tends to collapse unaccountably in moments of crisis. Kay hung gay curtains in front of a set of old oak book-shelves and made them into a shoe rack: thereby combining utility with an illusory air of culture. No small achievement.

The inner wall opposite the window, which used to be the outside wall of the house, is an interesting pattern of weathered ships' beams and brick. The new walls are done in white and the concrete floor in red.

Altogether it is an agreeable kitchen, and we find ourselves spending more time in it than we had bargained for. It is the heart of the house, as perhaps a kitchen should be. Looking at the old shack from outside you could not possibly deduce its existence.

But the very virtues that make it so cosy and inviting in winter also make it insufferable in a really high summer. Apart from the vast acreage of glass which turns it into a greenhouse, it contains The Boiler. This device, squat and smug in its sheath of vitreous enamel, heats the water as well as the kitchen. If we are to maintain the minimum civilized standard of hygiene – Kay's minimum: I could manage on a good deal less – we have to keep the monster fed day and night throughout the year. Quite apart from the toil and dust and the fearful expense, from noon onwards on a warm day the kitchen is unbearable.

Now the propaganda which Kay has been putting out for years at last bears fruit. I, who can bear others' sufferings in the lovely cold weather with equanimity, am beaten by the heat.

The general plan falls into two parts. Shade will be provided by one of those gay striped roll-down awnings which you see outside shops and cafés here and there on the Continent. Hot water will be provided in summer by an immersion heater. So far, so good. But what becomes of the boiler and how do we heat the kitchen in winter? At this point Kay leaves me far behind, marvelling at the reckless courage and resourcefulness of the weaker sex. It appears that we have three courses open to us.

(1) We tear out the slow combustion stove which heats the living room and replace it by a crafty affair which will keep radiators going all over the house.

(2) We replace the kitchen boiler by one which will supply radiators all over the house.

(3) We go all-electric.

Kay has worked out the cost in money with an accountant's painstaking pessimism. That is bad enough, in all conscience. But what makes me flinch is the certain knowledge that any scheme will involve tearing out a few hundred feet of piping and re-plumbing the house from top to bottom. However, Kay and old Wally have persuaded themselves that it will be an interesting way of passing the time during the dark days. So I suppose I have to put a good face on it. However, behind the complacent mask I wear lurks a resolve as implacable as their own. As a procrastinator I have the advantage over Kay and Wally: a lifetime's practice and training have made me positively Machiavellian when it comes to concealing the no behind the yes. We shall stagger on from discussion to discussion. After all, it is better to travel hopefully than to arrive. I have little doubt that I can wear them down.

(And I did. In the end we compromised on a system of Dimplex oil-fired electric radiators, costly to run but positively the most labour-saving device of all.)

6

Envoy

So autumn comes round again, and the household settles down to the long half of the year. Spring and summer pass so swiftly, with all their sensuous pleasures and deceptive intimations: borne up on their fragrances and on the flattering English light, one is a little drunk with consciousness, and life stretches ahead as if illimitable. In an English garden on any decent day between April and September, I mean a day warm enough for shirt sleeves and summer dresses, warm enough to sit down for a rest and a drink between the little bouts of work, then one feels at one's best, tranquil but alert, vivacious yet dependable. It is in summer that we plan our books, and nothing seems impossible. Communication is in the air, the mysteries are all about to be revealed. At one with the insects and the birds, flattered by the flowers, we feel the verity of creation flowing, irresistible. It is when the reckoning comes, back in the study, back by the fireside, once more a child of lamplight, that the vitality ebbs in the vein, the secrets we were about to peel apart close up, forever impenetrable. . . .

Man is a poet or he is nothing. Most of us manage at some time to express some tiny fraction of our poetic apprehension, in our work or our play or our loving, and to the degree that we are frustrated in this expression, we are frustrated in the innermost recesses of our being. A cottage life is essentially poetic: what one conjures up out of the raw materials of living is a framework of creative routine within which the spirit or soul can flower harmoniously. True, it does not suit every sort of soul. There are born cottagers (many of whom happen not to be born in cottages) and there are born townsfolk, to whom the country is at best empty, at worst intimidating. I know many people who are incapable of living the cottage life: some who find it merely boring in its apparent uneventfulness, some who find it rather hostile. To live happily in a country cottage, especially a remote one, calls for a certain sort of placid acceptance of the natural creation, which as a people we seem to be breeding out. Yet there are enough, I fancy, who respond to the lure of the self-contained yet really wonderfully interdependent life of the cottage to make estate agents quite happy, and this state of affairs will doubtless continue for some time to come.

As I write, it is now exactly twenty years since we left London to live in Tea-Cosy Cottage, and we have also lived for a shorter spell in another cottage, a really remote one, deeply hidden down a rutted and winding track, with its back to the dark woods of the Sussex Weald, and not a chimney visible from its windows. We left this cottage only because we had no choice, or *thought* we had no choice: one of those all-too-human decisions which, in retrospect, reflect rather badly on one's capacity for rational thought. Now, after a few years spent in a bungalow half-hidden in its thicket or spinney of oak and ash, beech and blackthorn, on the fringe of a one-time village that has been 'developed' into a sort of incomplete and ambiguous town, we are contemplating our final move – surely it will be final – back once more to a cottage in the veritable country.

I find myself strangely but happily indifferent to the details of the choice before us. So long as it is a habitable and tranquil cottage, with a strong possibility around it of creating the sort of garden we have come to recognize as our congenial bower – many beautiful and varied shrubs, a complex and secretive interlacing of boughs and leaves, many climbing and creeping growths, a plenitude of trees – then frankly I do not greatly mind whether it be by this river or that lake, in this valley or that sequestered combe. But that it shall be handy for the trout-inhabited water is the first condition, or very nearly the first. I may spend very little time casting a fly, but I want to spend many hours still and silent at the waterside, especially in spring, breathing in that exhilarating sense of renewal and tranquillity which inhabits those loveliest of all locations, 'where the bright waters meet'.

It may again be timbered Tudor beamy, like Tea-Cosy; or Regency demure, like the Sussex cottage. It may be Cotswold stone. It may be tile-hung. It may be thatched, tiled, or roofed with slabs of hoary stone. It will surely have little windows, a number of them, diamond-latticed; and a porch with honey-suckle or clematis entwined about it. I hope it will have an ample kitchen with a Rayburn or Aga, where a man can sit and eat and drink and pull off his boots and relax. It is time to relax. And the place to relax, for me at any rate, is a country cottage, with the right woman and the right water, and all around you the well-wooded, well-watered countryside of essential England. We shall find it, one fine day, and once again, it will be like coming home. For home is where the heart is.